John C. D. Thompson

Thompson's Hotel Directory and Travelers' Guide to the United States

John C. D. Thompson

Thompson's Hotel Directory and Travelers' Guide to the United States

ISBN/EAN: 9783337211288

Printed in Europe, USA, Canada, Australia, Japan

Cover: Foto ©Lupo / pixelio.de

More available books at **www.hansebooks.com**

THOMPSON'S
HOTEL DIRECTORY

---AND---

Travelers' Guide to the United States.

GIVING AN ACCURATE LIST OF HOTELS, CITIES AND
TOWNS, RAILROADS AND OTHER INFORMATION
OF A VALUABLE NATURE TO THE
TRAVELING PUBLIC.

---TO WHICH HAS BEEN ADDED AN---

Advertising Directory and Buyers' Guide,

REPRESENTING THE LEADING MANUFACTURERS AND
BUSINESS HOUSES OF THE COUNTRY.

PRICE, - - - 50 CENTS.

PUBLISHED AND COMPILED BY

J. C. D. THOMPSON, No. 109 LIBERTY STREET,

New York.

PREFATORY.

I have the pleasure of presenting to my patrons and the public the first issue of THOMPSON'S HOTEL DIRECTORY AND TRAVELERS' GUIDE.

It was commenced about six months ago, and has been pushed forward as rapidly as the magnitude of the undertaking would permit. No one who is not familiar with similar works can conceive of the amount of labor and the great expense attached to such a publication.

The plan and arrangement is entirely original, and it is to-day the *only* work of its kind. In compiling it, great care has been taken to make it as *plain* as possible, so that the information it contains can be seen at a glance, and be easily referred to.

My long experience as a publisher and past success has enabled me to present such a valuable book, and I trust that it will meet with the approval and success it justly merits. I thank my many patrons for the great encouragement given me, and trust the work will meet with your approval.

Finally, I call special notice to the ADVERTISING DIRECTORY AND BUYER'S GUIDE "department," where are represented many of the largest manufacturers and business firms in the United States.

THE PUBLISHER.

GEORGE C. BEDELL.   JAMES M. JARVIS.

GEO. C. BEDELL & CO.

General Mercantile

PRINTERS

Stationers, Etc.

109 LIBERTY STREET,

New York City

Hotel ✣ Brighton,

Broadway, 42d St. and Seventh Ave.,

NEW YORK.

Cars from Grand Central and West Shore Railway Stations direct to the Hotel, 20 minutes from Wall St. by Elevated R. R.

SUPERIOR ACCOMMODATIONS FOR FAMILIES AND GENTLEMEN.

Excellent Restaurant at Moderate Prices.

A. DUGUID & CO., Props.

WESTERN ✢ UNION ✢ HOTEL,

Cor. West and Cortlandt Streets, New York.

Ticket Agents for all Steamships and Railways.

Board and Lodging by the Day or Week.

DRAFTS at lowest rates, payable in any part of Great Britain. Sovereigns bought and sold.

To prevent loss, money sent to this house should be by POST OFFICE ORDER.

Persons intending to travel to any part of the United States or to Europe, by writing to this house in advance, will be met on arrival in New York. Before purchasing tickets it will be advantageous to first consult the proprietors, and thereby secure the CHEAPEST and MOST DIRECT ROUTE to destination.

This Hotel is located directly opposite the Pennsylvania Railroad Station; is five minutes' walk from the Erie Railway Depot, Castle Garden, Liverpool Steamship Dock, and one block from Washington Market, which makes it the most convenient hotel in New York City for travelers. ☞ *OPEN DAY AND NIGHT.* ☜

Pains will be taken to receive all the best Mining information at this house

Terms: Board and Lodging, $7 per week. Single Meals, 35 cts.

MARTIN & WILLS, Proprietors.

THOMPSON'S
HOTEL DIRECTORY AND TRAVELERS' GUIDE

ABERDEEN, Miss. Situa'ed on the Tombigbee River. Population, 2,400.

Hotels—European, **Gordon House, City.**

ADRIAN, Mich. Situated on the River Raisin. Population, 9,000.

Hotels—Central ($2.00 per day), **Lawrence House.**

AKRON, O. Population, 16,512. *Railroads*—Cleveland, Mt. Vernon & Delaware; New York, Pennsylvania & Ohio—occupy same depot; Pitts., Cleveland & Toledo; Valley—have separate depots. *Business interests*—Manufacturing and mercantile.

Hotels—**Windsor, New Sumner House, Cascade House, Hotel Buctel, Clariden, Empire House** ($2.00 per day).

ALBANY, Ga. Situated on the Flint River, at the head of navigation. Population, 3050.

Hotels—**Barnes' Albany House, Bogen House.**

ALBANY, N. Y. Situated on both banks of the Hudson, which is here crossed by two double-track railroad bridges. Population, 90,903. The New York Central & Hudson River R. R. and Boston & Albany R. R. share the union station one block from the depot of the New York, West Shore & Buffalo, and Delaware & Hudson

---

For advertising space in this work address the National Directory Co., New York City.

Canal Co.'s R. R. (Susquehanna & Saratoga Division). The new state capitol at Albany (modeled after the Louvre Palace), which will be one of the finest granite buildings in the world, has been building twelve years and covers three and one-half acres of land, with a projected height of 384 feet. It has cost upwards of $11,-000,000. One mile southwest of the city are the buildings of the State Insane and Fever Hospitals, and the Industrial School. Albany is the centre of a lucrative commercial trade and the seat of large stove factories, shoe shops, breweries, etc.

Hotels—**Delavan, Kenmore.**

ALBIA, Iowa. Population, 2,391.
Hotel—**Cramer House.**

ALBION, N. Y. Located on the Erie Canal. Population, 4,204.
Hotels—**Orleans House** ($2 per day), **Albion House, Exchange Hotel.**

ALEXANDRIA, Va. Situated on the Potomac River, seven miles below Washington, D. C. A port of entry. Population, 13,658. *Railroads*—Baltimore & Potomac; Virginia Midland; Washington, Ohio—all roads occupy separate depots. *Business interests*—Mercantile.
Hotels—**Mansion, Alexandria, Tontine.**

ALLENTOWN, Pa. Situated on the Lehigh River. Population, 20,000. *Railroads*—Central of New Jersey; Lehigh Valley; Philadelphia & Reading—all roads occupy separate depots. Philadelphia & Reading and Lehigh Valley connect at East Pennsylvania Junction. *Business interests*—Manufacturing (iron) and mercantile.
Hotels—**American, Allen House, Kramer House.**

This work is circulated gratuitously among prominent hotels of the United States.

MAC URQUARHT'S

Worcestershire Sauce.

Manuf'red and Bottled in England.

In England there are many brands of Worcestershire Sauce, and none stand higher than Mac Urquarht's, as it it one of the oldest and best known Sauces throughout England and her Colonies. It is pronounced by connoisseurs superior in every respect to any Sauce offered, and is rapidly usurping the market in the United States.

The following certificate from one of the best known English Chemists sufficiently proves that it is perfectly pure and wholesome:

"The condiment's and materials used in Messrs. MAC URQUARHT & Co.'s Worcestershire Sause are perfectly pure and of exceptional quality, and the sauce is entirely free from mineral or other noxious ingredients."

"BENJ. NICKELS, F.C.S., F.I.C.,
"*Analytical and Technical Chemist, London, England.*"

From a comparison of the prices MAC URQUARHT'S is some 20 per cent. cheaper than Lee & Perrin's.

Leading Hotels and Restaurants in New York City—a class of trade that always demand the BEST of everything—now use Mac Urquarht's Sauce. Why can't you?

We invite a trial order from the trade generally.

Beach & Sherwood, 139 & 141 Franklin St., N.Y.
SOLE AGENTS FOR THE UNITED STATES.

BORSUM BROS.

UNIVERSAL METAL POLISHING PASTE—
PUTZ-POMADE—

TRUMPINE.

THE GENUINE.

THE ORIGINAL!

UNIVERSAL·METAL·POLISHING·PASTE
TRUMPINE
TRADE MARK.
·BORSUM·BROS·N·Y·
Take a little on soft cloth, rub the metal hard; clean off, then rub with dry CLEAN cloth.

THE VERY BEST.

TRY IT !!

The Finest in the World for producing a Brilliant and lasting Polish without scratching. It is labor-saving, cheap and in convenient form for use, and has no equal for Polishing Brass, Copper, Nickel, German Silver, Zinc, Tin, etc. *Free from acid, alkali and grit.*

BORSUM BROS.

IMPORTERS AND MANUFACTURERS,

91 CLIFF STREET, NEW YORK.

SAMPLES SENT FREE ON APPLICATION.

ALLEGHENY CITY, Pa. Situated on the Allegheny River, opposite Pittsburg, Pa. Population, 78,681. *Railroads*—Pennsylvania (West Penna. Div.); Pittsburg, Fort Wayne & Chicago—depots opposite on same street; Pittsburg & Western—occupies separate depot. *Business interests*—Manufacturing (iron) and mercantile. Location of the Western Pennsylvania Penitentiary.
Hotel—**Central.**
ALLIANCE, O. Situated on the Mahoning River. Population, 4633.
Hotels—**Arlington, Chase, Sourbeck, Union.**
ALTOONA, Pa. Population, 19,719. *Railroad*—Pennsylvania (Main Line and Hollidaysburg & Newry Branch). *Business interest*—Manufacturing. The Pennsylvania Railroad shops are located here. The city is situated at the east base of the Allegheny mountains, where the road begins to ascend. The road in its ascent between Altoona and Cresson winds around the side of the mountain, affording some of the finest mountain scenery on the continent. Here also is the famous Horse Shoe Bend.
Hotels—**Logan House, Globe, Central, Arlington, Brant House.**
ALTON, Ill. Situated on the Mississippi River, ten miles above the mouth of the Missouri River. Population, 9500.
Hotel—**Madison.**
AMERICUS, Ga. Population 3879.
Hotels—**Commercial, Barlow.**
AMESBURY, Mass. Situated on and near the mouth of Merrimack River. Population, 3341.

For advertising space in this work address the National Directory Co., New York City.

Hotel—American House.

AMHERST, N. S. Situated near an inlet of Chignecto Bay. Population, 4000.
Hotels—Lamey's Dominion, Terrace.

AMSTERDAM, N. Y. Situated on the Mohawk River. The Erie Canal is opposite. Population, 11,711. *Railroad*—New York Central & Hudson River. *Business interests*—Manufacturing.
Hotels—Brunswick, Commercial, City, Central, German.

ANDOVER, Mass. Population, 5070.
Hotels—Mansion House, Elm House.

ANNAPOLIS, Md. Situated on Chesapeake Bay at the mouth of Severn River. Population, 6500.
Hotels—City, Maryland, Carroll House.

ANN ARBOR, Mich. Situated upon both sides of the Huron River. Population, 8500.
Hotels—Cook's, Leonard House, St. James.

APPLETON, Wis. Situated on the Lower Fox River. Population, 8005.
Hotels—Waverly House, Briggs House.

ASHLAND, Pa. Population, 6014.
Hotels—Union, Locust Mountain, Mansion, Ashland, American.

ASTORIA, Ore. Situated at the mouth of the Columbia River. Population, 6500.
Hotels—Occident, Parker House.

ATCHISON, Kan. Situated on the Missouri River. Population, 15,106. *Railroads*—Atchison, Topeka & Santa Fe; Chicago, Rock Island & Pacific; Central Branch

This work is circulated gratuitously among prominent hotels of the United States.

THE STANLEY WORKS,

NEW BRITAIN, CONN.

Butt, Hinge and Bolt Works.   Tack and Nail Works.

Warehouse, 79 Chambers Street, New York.

AMERICAN BARB FENCE WIRE,

PAINTED OR GALVANIZED.

THIS WIRE contains six times as many Barbs per foot as any other, and is the only Fence that is as efficient against small as against large animals. It will not slip through the Staple, and is the only Barb Wire that is GALVANIZED AFTER IT IS FINISHED, which adds greatly to its strength and durability. This Wire is made on an entirely different principle from any other, is amply secured by Letters Patent, and no infringement upon any other Patent Right.

Sample of Wire and Prices sent upon application. Mention THE HOTEL GUIDE when writing.

AMERICAN FENCING COMPANY,

OFFICE: No. 234 WEST 29TH STREET, NEW YORK.

WORKS: { Nos. 232, 234, 236, 238 West 29th Street.
Nos. 225, 227, 229, 231, 233, 235, 237, 239 West 28th Street.

Missouri Pacific; Hannibal & St. Joseph; Kansas City, St. Joseph & Council Bluffs—occupy same depot; Atchison & Nebraska; Missouri Pacific—occupy same depot; Central Branch Missouri Pacific—has also a separate depot. Free transfer for through passengers between separate depots. *Business interests*—Manufacturing and mercantile.

Hotel—**The New Byram** ($2.50 and $3 per day).

ATHENS, Ga. Situated on the Oconee River. Population 5870.

Hotel—**Newton House.**

ATLANTA, Ga. Population, 34,398. Capital of State, and one of the most important cities in the South. *Railroads*—Richmond & Danville; A. & C. Air-Line Div.; Atlanta & West Point; Georgia; Central of Georgia; Western & Atlantic; Georgia Pacific—all roads occupy Union Depot. *Business interests*—Manufacturing, mercantile and agricultural.

Hotels—**Markham House, Kimball House.**

ATLANTIC CITY, N. J. Situated on the Atlantic Ocean, fifty-eight miles from Philadelphia. Population, 5478.

Hotels—**United States, Brighton, Congress Hall, Surf, Chalfonte, Mansion, Dennis' Seaside, Ocean.**

ATTLEBORO, Mass. Intersected by Mill River. Population, 11,111. *Railroads*—Boston & Providence; Old Colony—occupy same depot. *Business interests*—Manufacturing jewelry, &c.

Hotel—**Ryder House.**

AUBURN, Me. Situated on the Androscoggin River. Population, 9600.

For advertising space in this work address the National Directory Co., New York City.

Hotels—**Elm, Maine, Lake Auburn.**

AUBURN, N. Y. Situated two and one-half miles Northwest of Owasco Lake, the outlet of which flows through the town. Population, 21,924. *Railroads*—New York Central & Hudson River; Southern Central: Ithaca, Auburn & Western—occupy separate depots. *Business interests*—Manufacturing and mercantile.

Hotels—**Osborne House, Gaylord House, National Hotel.**

AUGUSTA, Ga. Situated on the Savannah River. Population, 23,023. In the vicinity are many localities of interest to the tourist and pleasure seeker. *Railroads*—Central of Georgia; Charlotte, Columbia & Augusta; Georgia; Port Royal & Augusta; South Carolina—all occupy same depot. *Business interests*—Cotton, mercantile and manufacturing.

Hotels—**Planters', Augusta, Globe, Central.**

AUGUSTA, Me. Situated on the Kennebec River, forty-five miles above its mouth. Population, 8682.

Hotels—**Augusta House, Cony House, Hotel North.**

AURORA, Ill. Situated on both banks of the Fox River. Population, 11,825. *Railroads*—Chicago & Iowa; Chicago, Burlington & Quincy (three divisions)—occupy same depot. *Business interests*—Manufacturing. Location of the Chicago, Burlington & Quincy car, machine and repair shops.

Hotels—**Hotel Evans, Empire, Tremont, Huntoon.**

AUSTIN, Texas. Capital. Situated on the Colorado River. Population, 10,960. *Railroads*—Houston & Texas Central; International & Great Northern—occupy same depot; Austin & Northwestern—in separate depot. *Bus-*

This work is circulated gratuitously among prominent hotels of the United States.

EUROPEAN PLAN.

Union Square Hotel & Hotel Dam

Union Square and 15th Street,

NEW YORK.

A. J. DAM & SON,
PROPRIETORS.

Rooms, $1.50 and Upward per Day.

THE
Park Avenue Hotel.

Occupying the entire front, between 32d and 33d Streets, on Fourth Avenue, and covering half the block in depth to Madison Avenue, its location is most central for transient visitors, and families desiring the quietude of an elegant home—contiguous to the most fashionable thoroughfares, and with means of quick conveyance to all business centres. Within eight minutes walk of the Grand Central Depot, from which trains depart and arrive from all points, and within five minutes' walk of either the West-side or East-side Elevated Railroads.

As a structure it is absolutely the only fire proof hotel building in the United States, and its Grand Parlor, eight Reception Rooms, Library, Dining Rooms, and five hundred Sleeping Rooms, with connecting Bathing and Dressing Rooms, are by a most systematic method thoroughly ventilated.

Surrounding a spacious Court, with Fountain, Summer Garden, Balconies and Electric Light. All its interior Rooms are most pleasant, while outside ones on its upper floors give extensive views of the East River, Long Island and the suburbs.

Ventilating Shafts intersect at each corner of its seven wide corridors, giving a continuous circulation of pure air throughout the building.

A number of Family Suites, with connecting Bathing Rooms, have been added this season.

The Hotel is conducted on the American system, and dispatches for accommodations will receive every attention.

$4.00 PER DAY.

HENRY CLAIR, Lessee.

iness interests—Mercantile and agricultural (cotton). Location of General Land Office of Texas.
Hotels—**Raymond House, Avenue, City, Brunswick, Southern.**

BALLSTON, N.Y. Population, 3,300.
Hotels—**Sans Souci, Medbery's, American, Ballston Spa House, Commercial, Eagle, Milton House.**

BALTIMORE, Md. Situated on the Patapsco River, twelve miles from its entrance into Chesapeake Bay. A port of entry. Population, 332,190. *Railroads*—Baltimore & Potomac; Northern Central; Philadelphia, Wilmington & Baltimore; Western Maryland — occupy Union Depot on Charles street; Baltimore & Potomac and Northern Central also occupy depots on Calvert street; Baltimore & Ohio, depot at Camden Station; Philadelphia, Wilmington & Baltimore, depot on President street; transfer without change of cars between President street and Camden Station for through trains; Western Maryland also occupy separate depots. *Business interests*—Shipping, manufacturing, commercial and mercantile.
Hotels—**Carrollton** ($4, $3.50 and $2.50 per day), **Barnum's, Maltby** (European plan, 75c. to $1.50 per day; American plan, $2 to $2.50 per day), **Eutaw, Rennert's, Mount Vernon, Mansion, Pepper's, Reilly's, Howard, Guy's.**

BANGOR, Me. Situated on the Penobscot River. Population, 16,857. *Railroads*—European & North American; Maine Central; Eastern Maine—occupy separate depots. *Business interests*—Lumber and manufacturing.

For advertising space in this work address the National Directory Co., New York City.

Hotels—**Bangor, Bangor Exchange, Franklin, Penobscot Exchange.**

BATAVIA, Ill. Situated on the Fox River. Population, 5,000.

Hotels—**Revere House, Totman House.**

BATAVIA, N. Y. Situated on the Tonawanda Creek. Population, 7,500.

Hotels **St. James, Washburn House, Hooper House, Park Hote', Ellicott House, Genesee House.**

BATH, Me. Situated on the Kennebec River. Population, 7,881.

Hotels—**Bath, Sagadahoc House, Columbian House, Sherman House, Central House, Commercial House.**

BATTLE CREEK, Mich. Situated on the Kalamazoo River, at the mouth of Battle Creek. Population, 7,000.

Hotels—**Williams, Lewis.**

BAY CITY, Mich. Four miles from head of Saginaw Bay, on Saginaw River, opposite West Bay City. Population, 20,693. *Railroads*—Detroit & Bay City, and Michigan Central—occupy same depot; Flint & Pere Marquette—separate depot.

Hotels—**Frazier House, Campbell House.**

BAY ST. LOUIS. Miss. Situated at mouth of Bay St. Louis, on Gulf of Mexico. Resident population, 1,978; transient, 8,000.

Hotel—**The Crescent.**

BELFAST, Me. Situated on Penobscot Bay. Population, 5,308.

Hotels—**American, New England House, Phœnix House.**

This work is circulated gratuitously among prominent hotels of the United States.

)PEAN PLANS.

Sta
No s a residence for families, or for
tourists, t
Pat entral Depot free of charge.

HAMMOND,

Fold-out Placeholder

BELLAIRE, O. Situated on the Ohio River, four and a half miles below Wheeling, W. Va. Population, 8,000.
Hotels—**Belmont, Globe, National, American.**

BELLEFONTAINE, O. Population, 4,400.
Hotels—**Metropolitan, Logan, Depot.**

BELLEVILLE, Ill. Situated on Richland Creek. Population, 10,682. *Railroads*—Illinois & St. Louis; St. Louis, Alton & Terre Haute; Louisville & Nashville; Belleville & O'Fallon; Belleville and East Carondelet—occupy separate depots. *Business interests*—Manufacturing and agricultural.
Hotels—**Belleville, National, Thomas House, Hinckley House, Aberer's, Tiemann.**

BELLEVILLE, Ont. Situated on Bay of Quinte. Population, 10,500. *Railroads*—Grand Trunk, Midland of Canada. *Business interests*—Lumber and manufacturing.
Hotels—**Dafoe House, Queen's, Dominion, Commercial.**

BELLVILLE, N. J. Population, 3,000.
Hotel—**Mansion House.**

BELLVILLE, Texas. Population, 600.
Hotels—**Harlaff, City, Manning.**

BELLOWS FALLS, Vt. Situated on the Connecticut River. Population, 3,799.
Hotels—**Towns', Island House.**

BELOIT, Wis. Situated on the Rock River. Population, 5,000,
Hotels—**Goodwin House, Commercial.**

For advertising space in this work address the National Directory Co., New York City.

BENNINGTON, Vt. Population, 3,400.
Hotels—**Stark House, Elm Tree House, Putnam.**

BETHLEHEM, Pa. Situated on both sides of the Lehigh River. Population, 5,000.
Hotels—**Eagle, Sun, American. Pacific, Central, Washington.**

BEVERLY, Mass. Population, 7,865.
Hotels—**Wallace, Careys', Railroad.**

BIDDEFORD, Me. Situated on the Saco River. Population, 12,652. *Railroads*—Boston & Maine; Eastern —occupy separate depots. *Business interests*—Manufacturing.
Hotels—**Biddeford House.**

BINGHAMPTON, N. Y. Population, 17,315. *Railroads*—Delaware & Hudson Canal Co. (Susquehanna Division); New York, Lake Erie & Western; Delaware, Lackawanna & Western—occupy separate Depots. *Business interests*—Manufacturing and mercantile; also fast becoming a fashionable summer resort.
Hotels—**Bennett, Crandall, Exchange, Lewis House.**

BIRMINGHAM, Ala. Population, 4,050.
Hotels—**Relay House, Kentucky House, Nixon's, St. Charles, Central, Richards.**

BISMARCK, Dak. Situated on line of Northern Pacific Railroad and East bank of Missouri River.
Hotels—**Sheridan, Merchants, Custer, Western.**

BLACK RIVER FALLS, Wis. Situated on the Black River and is the headquarters of a very extensive lumber interest. Population, 1427.
Hotel—**Lake's.**

This work is circulated gratuitously among prominent hotels of the United States.

EARLE'S HOTEL,
Cor. Canal and Centre Streets,
Near Broadway,   NEW YORK.

ON THE AMERICAN AND EUROPEAN PLAN.

One of the Best Hotels in the lower part of the City for the Traveling Public. Elegant in Appointments, Centrally Located and Most Economical in Prices.

IMPORTANT.—Travelers and Families arriving or leaving the City for business, pleasura, or to visit summer resorts, will find superior accommodations at this Hotel. Guests on arriving save $2.60 carriage hire, by handing their Baggage Checks to Express Agent and taking street cars direct to Hotel.

Acknowledged by the Fire Dep't to be the Safest in case of Fire

Room and Board, - - $2.50 per Day.
Rooms (only) $1.00 per Day and Upward.

NEW AUTOMATIC PASSENGER ELEVATOR.
FRENCH, GERMAN AND SPANISH SPOKEN.

FERD. P. EARLE, Owner and Proprietor.

Now open, the most complete and comfortable Hotel in New York.

THE NEW AND PALATIAL
HOTEL NORMANDIE
Cor. Broadway and 38th Street.

On the European Plan, with a Restaurant of Peculiar Excellence.

ESTERBROOK, Inspector of Buildings, says: "Every room is a place of security for its occupant as the entire house is absolutely fire-proof."

Steam heat, speaking tubes, electric bells, burglar and fire alarms attached to all rooms.

Sanitary arrangements perfect. Location the most Healthy in the City.

Special attention to Weddings, Receptions and Dinner Parties. Liberal arrangements to Permanent Guests.

ROOMS $2 PER DAY AND UPWARDS.   FERD. P. EARLE, PROPRIETOR

BLACKSTONE, Mass. Situated on the Blackstone River. Population. 4937.
Hotels **Union, Lincoln.**
BLOOMINGTON, Ill. Population, 17,184. *Railroads*—Chicago & Alton; Indiana, Bloomington & Western; Lake Erie & Western—occupy same depot. Illinois Central—occupies separate depot. *Business interests*—Agricultural. Location of the State Normal University, the Wesleyian University and the Chicago & Alton R. R. car, machine and repair shops.
Hotels—**Ashley, Phœnix.**
BLOOMSBURG, Pa. Situated on Fishing Creek and North Branch of the Susquehanna River. Population, 3704.
Hotels—**American, City, Exchange, Central, Railroad House.**
BOONE, Ia. Situated on an elevated rolling prairie two miles from the Des Moines River. Population, 3313.
Hotels—**Lincoln, Eagle, St. James.**
BOONEVILLE, Mo. Situated on the Missouri River. Population, 3855.
Hotel—**City.**
BORDENTOWN, N. J. Situated on the Delaware River at the southern terminus of the Delaware and Raritan Canal. Population, 6003.
Hotels—**American, City, Washington, Bordentown.**
BOSTON, Mass. Population, 362,535. *Railroads*—Boston & Albany; Boston & Maine; Boston & Providence; Boston & Lowell; Boston, Revere Beach & Lynn; Eastern; Fitchburg; New York & New England; Old Colony—all roads occupy separate depots, except the

---

For advertising space in this work address the National Directory Co., New York City.

Moonsocket Div. of New York and New England, which occupies the Boston & Albany depot. *Business interests*— Manufacturing and commercial.

Hotels—**Adams, American, Brunswick, Clarendon, Crawford, Milliken, Revere, Tremont, United States, Young's, Parker House.**

BOWLING GREEN, Ky. Situated on the Big Barren River at the head of navigation. Population, 4895.
Hotels—**American, Merchants', Morehead House, Potter House.**

BRADFORD, Pa. Population, 9197.
Hotels—**St. James, Henderson, Riddell, Burt, Aiken.**

BRANFORD, Fla. Population, 500. Terminus of Branford Branch of the Savannah, Florida & Western R. R., and head of navigation on the Suwannee River, connecting with steamer "Caddo Bell" Tuesdays and Fridays for Cedar Keys and Key West, thence to the West Indies and Mexican Gulf port.
Hotel—**Branford House.**

BRANTFORD, Ont. Situated on the Grand River. Population, 11,000. *Railroads*—Great Western of Canada, and its Brantford, Norfolk & Port Burwell Branch —occupy same depot; Grand Trunk occupies separate depot. *Business interests*—Mercantile and manufacturing.
Hotels—**American, Commercial, Kirby House.**

BRENHAM, Texas. Population, 4200.
Hotels—**Central, Exchange, Pennington.**

BRIDGEPORT, Ct. Situated on an islet of Long Island Sound, at the mouth of the Pequonnock River. Population, 29,148. *Railroads*—Housatonic; Naugatuck,

This work is circulated gratuitously among prominent hotels of the United States.

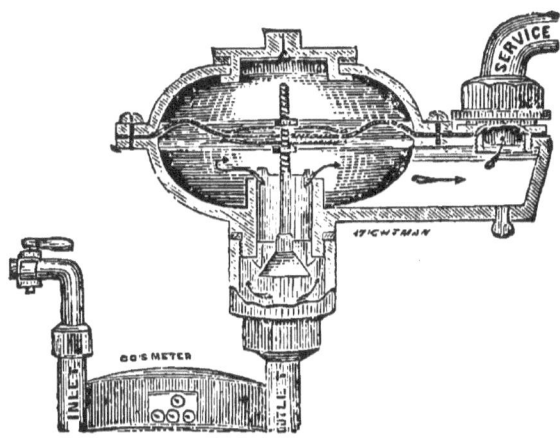

ACCURATE! **RELIABLE!** **PROVED BY EXPERIENCE.**

SAVE YOUR MONEY, REDUCE YOUR GAS BILLS
WITHOUT REDUCING YOUR LIGHT.

Apply to

THE GAS SAVING COMPANY,
169 Broadway, New York.

This apparatus is in use on the **GOVERNMENT BUILDINGS** in **WASHINGTON, D. C.**, and was adopted after severe competitive tests. Among a large number of New York references are:

THE EQUITABLE LIFE ASSURANCE SOCIETY.
GRAND CENTRAL DEPOT
BAY STATE SHOE AND LEATHER CO.
OLD COLONY S. B. CO., FALL RIVER LINE
ATLAS STEAMSHIP CO., PIM, FORWOOD & CO.
D. APPLETON & CO.
THEO. L. DeVINNE & CO.
FRANK LESLIE'S   N. Y. HERALD.
THE CHURCHMAN   N. Y. OBSERVER.
THE U. S. NAVAL HOSPITAL, BROOKLYN

Send for Circulars.

20 to 50 per cent. saving guaranteed.

NO CHEMICALS USED.
NO GLYCERINE. NO MERCURY.

AGENTS WANTED IN GAS-BURNING TOWNS.

NEEDED IN EVERY HOTEL AND RESTAURANT.

New York, New Haven & Hartford—all occupying depot.
Business interests—Manufacturing and fisheries.
Hotels—**Atlantic** ($3 per day), **Sterling** ($2 per day), **Pequonnock** ($1.25 to $1.50 per day), **Golden Hill** ($1.50 to $1.75 per day), **Elm** ($1.50 per day).

BRIDGETON. N. J. Situated on both sides of the Cohansey River. Population, 8722.
Hotels—**City, Davis'**.

BRISTOL, Pa. Situated on the Delaware River, opposite Burlington, N. J., at the terminus of the Delaware Division Pennsylvania Canal. Population, 5474.
Hotels—**Cottage, Delaware, Classon House, Railroad House**.

BRISTOL, Tenn. Population. 3000.
Hotels—**Virginia, Thomas**.

BROCKVILLE. Ont. Situated on the St. Lawrence River. Population, 8500.
Hotel—**Reveie House**.

BROCKTON, Mass. Population, 13,608. *Railroad*—Old Colony. *Business interests*—Manufacturing boots and shoes.
Hotels—**Brockton House, Holbrook House, Winter's Hotel**.

BROOKLYN, N. Y. Situated on Long Island, New York Bay, opposite New York City. Population, 566,689. *Railroads*—Brooklyn, Bath & Coney Island; Long Island; Prospect Park & Coney Island; Pennsylvania & New York, West Shore & Buffalo—occupy same depot. *Business interests*—Manufacturing and mercantile. The city limits include Williamsburg and Bushwick.

For advertising space in this work address the Notional Directory Co., New York City.

Hotels--**Pierrepont House, Brooklyn Heights, Mansion House, Clinton House.**

BROWNSVILLE, Tenn. Population, 2475.
Hotels--**Exchange, Galt House.**

BRUNSWICK, Ga. Situated on St. Simon's Sound, at the mouth of the Turtle River. Population, 3500.
Hotel--**Nelson.**

BRYAN, Texas. Population, 2790.
Hotels--**Commercial House, Campbell House, Barnett House, Waldron House, Prima Vista.**

BUCYRUS, Ohio. Situated on the Sandusky River. Population, 4000.
Hotels--**Deal House, Monnett House, Western House.**

BUFFALO. N. Y. Situated at the eastern extremity of Lake Erie and the western terminus of the Erie Canal. Population, 155,137. *Railroads*--Buffalo, New York & Philadelphia; New York, West Shore & Buffalo; --occupy same depot; New York. Lake Erie & Western; Buffalo & Southwestern; Grand Trunk, Lehigh Valley--occupy same depot; New York Central & Hudson River; Lake Shore & Michigan Southern; Michigan Central (Canada Southern Division); New York, Chicago & St. Louis--occupy same depot; Delaware, Lackawanna & Western--has separate depot. *Business interests*--Commercial (grain, iron, leather, lumber, two large grape sugar manufactories).
Hotels--**Genesee, Tifit House, Mansion, Bloomer, Continental.**

BURLINGTON, Iowa. Situated on the Mississippi

This work is circulated gratuitously among prominent hotels of the United States.

WHAT'S TRUMPS?

Progressive Euchre and Whist Parties.

If you want something fine for favors or scoring get "HYATT'S PATENT GAME REGISTER AND TRUMP INDICATOR." Shows

TRUMP POINTS AND GAMES.

Made in several styles. Plain, Fancy, Hand-painted and Leather. Prices respectively 15 cents, 25 cents, 50 cents and $1. Sent by mail on receipt of price. The trade supplied.

On receipt of $1 will send, post-paid, two Indicators, fancy pattern; a pack of fine Cards and a Pocket Edition of Whist, by WM. POLE, F. R. S.

GEO. W. HYATT,

114 Nassau Street,   New York City.

THOMAS D. STETSON,

Solicitor of Patents

---AND---

EXPERT IN PATENT CASES,

No. 23 Murray St., New York.

CHAS. F. SCHMIDT & PETERS,

Importers of Fine Wines, &c.,

24 BEAVER ST., NEW YORK.

OSBORN & CO.,
Real ❋ Estate ❋ Brokers

AND PROPRIETORS OF THE

Original Arcade Servant Agency,

68 ARCADE, - - PROVIDENCE, R. I.

First-Class Male and Female Help furnished for Hotels, Boarding Houses, Restaurants, Private Families, &c.

River, 251 miles, by water, above St. Louis. Population, 19,450. *Railroads*—Burlington, Cedar Rapids & Northern; Burlington & Southwestern; Chicago, Burlington & Quincy, Main Line, Keokuk Division, and Quincy and Carthage Line; Wabash, St. Louis & Pacific—occupy same depot; Burlington & Northwestern (narrow gauge) separate depot. River steamers to St. Louis, St. Paul and intermediate landings. The residences upon the bluffs command a fine view of the river. *Business interests*—Manufacture and agricultural; good jobbing trade.

Hotels—**Gorham, Barrett, Union** ($2 per day).

BURLINGTON, N. J. Situated on the Delaware River, opposite Bristol, Pa. Population, 7655.
Hotels—**Belden's City, Atkinson's, Lutphen's.**

BURLINGTON, Vt. Situated on Burlington Bay, on the eastern shore of Lake Champlain. A port of entry. Population, 11,364. *Railroads*—Burlington and Lamoille, Central Vermont,—occupy same depot. *Business interests*—Lumber, marble and mercantile. The University of Vermont is located about a mile from the shore, at an elevation of 281 feet above the lake.

Hotels—**American, Van Ness House, Quincy House.**

CAIRO, Ill. Situated in the southern extremity of Illinois, at confluence of the Ohio and Mississippi Rivers. Population, 9017.
Hotels—**Halliday, St. Charles, Planters', Arlington.**

CAMBRIDGE. Mass. Situated near Charles River. Population, 52,740. *Railroads*—Boston & Lowell, Fitchburg. *Business interests*—Manufacturing. It is the

For advertising space in this work address the National Directory Co., New York City.

seat of Harvard University, the oldest, and one of the best in the United States, founded in 1638.
Hotels- **Porter's, Prospect House.**

CAMDEN, N. J. Situated on the Delaware River, opposite Philadelphia, by which it is connected by five ferries. Population, 41,658. *Railroads*—Pennsylvania (Amboy Div.); West Jersey—occupy same depot; Camden & Atlantic, Camden, Gloucester & Mt. Ephraim, Philadelphia & Atlantic City,—occupy separate depots. *Business interests*—Manufacturing, lumber trade, commercial, &c. The largest steel pen manufactory in the United States, that of Esterbrook & Co., is located here. Rapidly growing city.
Hotel—**West Jersey.**

CANANDAIGUA, N. Y. Situated on Lake Canandaigua. Population, 5679.
Hotels—**Seneca Point, Willow Grove, Woodville.**

CANTON, Ohio. Population, 20,000. *Railroads*—Pittsburg. Fort Wayne & Chicago, Valley, Connotton Valley. *Business interests*—Manufacturing and mercantile.
Hotels—**American, Ogden, St. Cloud.**

CANTON, Miss. Population, 2084.
Hotels—**Singleton House, City, European House.**

CAPE MAY, N. J. Situated on the Atlantic Ocean, at the entrance of Delaware Bay. Population, 2600.
Hotels—**Stockton, Congress Hall, Arctic, New Columbia, Windsor, Chalfonte, &c.**

CARBONDALE, Pa. Situated on the Lackawanna River, near its mouth. Population, 7814.
Hotels—**Harrison, American House.**

This work is circulated gratuitously among prominent hotels of the United States.

AUGUSTA HOUSE

State Street, Augusta, Maine.

Free Hacks to and from Depot & Steamboat

This popular house, recently refitted, renovated and refurnished is most pleasantly situated, overlooking the beautiful valley of the Kennebec; and, while it is adapted to the wants of the traveling public all the year round, it offers **SPECIAL INDUCEMENTS TO SUMMER TOURISTS**, who desire to spend the Summer pleasantly and amidst the most beautiful scenery in the State. The house has a perfect system of drainage, is supplied with pure spring water. The sleeping apartments are large and well ventilated, furnished in good style, hair matresses, etc. Electric Bells connect the rooms with the office. Gas in every room. The table will be supplied with the **BEST THE MARKET AFFORDS**, and prepared by experienced cooks, together with good attendance in the Dining Hall. The City of Augusta is the capital of the State, situated 60 miles from Portland and accessible by the Maine Central Railroad from Portland, running in connection with the Eastern Railroad from Boston. No change of cars. Or by steamer direct from Boston, which is a very pleasant route.

Excellent **FISHING, BOATING** and **GUNNING** are found here, and the drives are unexcelled. A **FIRST-CLASS LIVERY** will be kept to accommodate the public. The Maine Insane Hospital is located here, also the Soldiers' Home at Togus, the United States Arsenal, and other places of interest.

The proprietors, having had large experience in the hotel business, feel competent to cater to the public taste, and by efficient and accommodating management trust to have a fair share of the public patronage.

CHARLES MILLIKEN, Prop.

FRANK GREENE, Clerk.

Telephone and Telegraph Office in the House.

INTERNATIONAL HOTEL.

EUROPEAN PLAN.

17 & 19 PARK ROW,

Opposite New Post Office and Astor House

New York

Rooms, 75c., $1.00 and $2.00 per Day

J. VAN BRIMMER & CO.,

PROPRIETORS.

Billiard and Wine Room connected with Hotel.

CARLISLE, Pa. Population, 6198.
Hotels—Florence, Mansion, Thudrium, American, Pennsylvania, Washington, Letort, Gasber, Farmers and Drovers, Lerew, Franklin.

CARMI, Ill. Situated on the Little Wabash River. Population, 2522.
Hotel—Damron House.

CARTHAGE, Mo. Situated on the Spring River. Population, 4210.
Hotels—Karr's, Harrington's, City.

CATASAUQUA, Pa. Population, 3856.
Hotels—Mansion, American, Eagle, Catasauqua, Pennsylvania.

CEDAR FALLS, Ia. Situated on both sides of the Cedar River. Population, 3034.
Hotels—Davis, Commercial.

CEDAR RAPIDS, Ia. Situated near Cedar River. Population, 10,104. *Railroads*—Burlington, Cedar Rapids & Northern, Chicago & Northwestern,—occupy same depot; Chicago, Milwaukee & St. Paul, (Racine & South-western Div.) occupies separate depot. Several large pork-packing establishments and a number of flour mills give to the place considerable business activity.
Hotels—Grand, North-western, Pullman.

CENTRALIA, Ill. Population, 3644.
Hotels—Occidental, Centralia House.

CHAMBERSBURG, Pa. Situated on the Conococheague Creek. Population, 7500.

For advertising space in this work address the National Directory Co., New York City.

Hotels—Washington, National, Montgomery, Indian Queen Franklin.

CHAMPAIGN, Ill. Population. 5314.
Hotels—Moore House, Doane House, Scott House.

CHAMPLAIN, N. Y. Population. 1500.
Hotels—Champlain House, Mansion House, American House.

CHARITON, Ia. Situated on the Chariton River. Population, 2974.
Hotel—The Bates House.

CHARLESTON. S. C. Situated on a peninsula between the rivers Ashley and Cooper, which unite immediately below the town and form a spacious harbor, two miles in width, communicating with the ocean seven miles below. The largest city in South Carolina. Population, 49,999. *Railroads*—North-eastern, Savannah & Charleston,—occupy same depot; South Carolina—occupies separate depot. *Business interests*—Commercial. Among the places of interest in and about the city is White Point Garden and Magnolia Cemetery, which is one of the finest and largest cemeteries in the Southern States. A steamboat makes two trips to and from Sullivan's Island daily, affording visitors an opportunity of viewing the harbor, Fort Sumter, and other forts.
Hotels—Charleston, Pavilion, Waverly ($2.00 per day).

CHARLESTON, W. Va. Situated on the Great Kanawha River. Population, 4237.
Hotels—Hale, St. Albert.

CHARLOTTE, N. C. Situated on Sugar Creek. Population, 8612.

This work is circulated gratuitously among prominent hotels of the United States.

BARRETT & HOUSE

Long Acre Square,

Cor. Broadway & 43d St.   **NEW YORK CITY.**

European Plan

NEW HOUSE, ELEGANTLY FURNISHED

BARRETT & BROTHERS,

PROPRIETORS.

MADISON ✺ AVENUE ✺ HOTEL

Madison Ave. and 58th Street,

One Block from Central Park.   NEW YORK.

A ❧ First-Class ❧ Family ❧ Hotel,

CONDUCTED ON THE

AMERICAN PLAN

AT POPULAR PRICES.

W. M. HUMPHREY & CO., Proprietors.

Hotels—Central, Charlotte.

CHARLOTTESVILLE, Va. Situated on the Rivanna River. Population, 5000.
Hotels—Farrish, Central.

CHATHAM, Ont. Situated on the River Thames. Population, 8000.
Hotels—Garner, Rankin.

CHATTANOOGA, Tenn. Situated on the Tennessee River. Population, 12,892. *Railroads*—Alabama Great Southern; East Tennessee, Virginia & Georgia; Memphis & Charleston; Nashville, Chattanooga & St. Louis; Western & Atlantic; Cincinnati, New Orleans & Texas Pacific—all occupy the same depot. *Business interests*—Mercantile and iron manufacturing in all its branches, rolling mills, and blast furnaces. The river is navigable about ten months in the year, and for small boats at all times. The surrounding region is liberally supplied with water-power and timber, and the hills contain an abundance of coal and iron-ore. The principal object of interest in the vicinity is Lookout Mountain, three miles south of the town. Since the war, Lookout Mountain has become one of the best patronized resorts in the South. Upon the summit of the mountain, several miles in extent, are numerous hotels and cottages, affording ample accommodation for visitors. From Point Lookout, overlooking the town, the battle-field of Mission Ridge, the National Cemetery, and for many miles the course of the Tennessee River, is obtained one of the grandest views this country affords. Upon a fair day, prominent landmarks in seven States are plainly visible.

For advertising space in this work address the National Directory Co., New York City.

Hotels **Stanton House, Read House, Hamilton House, Stoops' European Hotel.**

CHELSEA, Mass. Population, 21,785. Suburb of Boston. *Railroad*—Eastern. *Business interests*—Manufacturing. Location of United States Marine Hospital.
Hotels—**Broadway House, City Hotel, Soldiers' Home.**

CHESTER, Pa. Situated on the Delaware River. Population, 14,996, *Railroads* Philadelphia, Wilmington & Baltimore; Philadelphia & Reading—separate depots. *Business interests* Manufacturing and iron ship-building. It is the oldest town in Pennsylvania, being settled by the Swedes in 1643.
Hotels **Washington, Columbia, City, Delaware, Brown's, American, Bea'e House.**

CHEYENNE, Wy. Situated on a broad open plain on Crow Creek, a small stream having its source in the Black Hills. Population, 4000.
Hotels **Inter-ocean, Dyer's, Union Pacific Railroad and Dining Room at Depot.**

CHICAGO, Ill. Situated on Lake Michigan at the mouth of Chicago River, and is also the eastern terminus of the Illinois and Michigan Canal. Population, 503,304. *Railroads*—Chicago & Alton; Pittsburg, Fort Wayne & Chicago; Chicago, Milwaukee & St. Paul; Chicago, St. Louis & Pittsburg; Chicago, Burlington & Quincy—occupy same depot; Illinois Central; Michigan Central;—occupy same depot; Chicago, Rock Island & Pacific; Lake Shore and Michigan Southern; New York, Chicago & St. Louis—occupy same depot; Chicago & Grand Trunk; Chicago & Eastern Illinois; Wabash, St. Louis

---

This work is circulated gratuitously among prominent hotels of the United States.

BELVEDERE HOUSE

— ON THE —

EUROPEAN PLAN.

Cor. Fourth Ave. and 18th St., N. Y.

(FORMERLY IRVING PLACE).

JOSEPH WEHRLE, Proprietor.

⚓ LELAND'S ⚓
STURTEVANT HOUSE

IS IN THE CENTER OF THE CITY,

BROADWAY (28th & 29th Sts.) NEW YORK

WITH ELEVATOR.

RATES REDUCED.—Rooms, with Board, $3,00 and $3.50 per Day, according to location.

Rooms on European Plan, $1.00 per day and upwards.

LELAND HOTEL,   WARREN F. LELAND,   CHICAGO, ILL.
LELAND HOTEL,   LELAND & WIGGINS,   SPRINGFIELD, ILL.
LELAND'S OCEAN HOTEL,   -   -   -   LONG BRANCH.
         CHARLES & WARREN LELAND, Jr.

L. & G. S. LELAND, Proprietors.

& Pacific; Chicago & Atlantic; Louisville, New Albany & Chicago--occupy same depot; Baltimore & Ohio; Chicago, Detroit & Niagara Falls Short Line—occupy same depot; Chicago & Northwestern—separate depot. Free transfer between all depots for through passengers. *Business interests*—All branches of business.

Hotels—**The Old Metropolitan Hotel**, 5th Avenue and Randolph Street (rates, $1.50 and $2.00 per day). **Astor House**, 73 and 75 Monroe Street (rates, $1.50 and $2.00 per day), C. A. Phillips proprietor. **Ogden House**, Washington and Franklin Streets (rates, $1.50 per day and up), D. Kelley & Son, proprietors. **Brigg's House**, (rates, $2.00 per day), Frank Upman, proprietor. **Palmer House**, American and European plans. Palmer House Co., Proprietors. **Gault House** (rates $2.00 and $2.50 per day). Hoyt & Gates, proprietors. **Sherman House** (rates, $3.00 and $3.50 per day), J. Irving Pearce, Proprietor. **The Commercial Hotel** (rates, $2.00 per day and up), Charles W. Dabb & Co., proprietors. **Washington Hotel** (rates, $2.00 per day and up), M. J. Henderson, proprietor. **The Continental** (terms, $2.00 and $2.50 per day), E. Hennessy, proprietor. **Matteson House** (rates, $2.50 and $3.00 per day), Munger Bros., proprietors. **Windsor European Hotel** (rates, 75 cents, $1.00, and $1.50 per day), Samuel Tregston, proprietor. **National Hotel**, 228 and 230 South Clark Street (rates, $1.50 to $2.00 per day), D. A. Dooley, proprietor. **Revere House**, Southeast corner Clark and Michigan Streets (terms, $2.00 per day and up). **Clifton House**, corner Wabash Avenue and Monroe Street (rates, $2.50 and $3.00 per day), Woodcock & Loring, proprietors. **Tremont House** (terms, $3.00 per day and up), John A.

For advertising space in this work address the National Directory Co., New York City.

Rice & Co., proprietors. **Farwell House,** corner Halsted and Jackson Streets (rates, $2.00 per day and up). **St. Charles Hotel,** 15 and 17 Clark Street (rates, $2.00 per day and up). Riggio Bros., proprietors. **Grand Pacific Hotel,** accommodation, 500 rooms, Drake, Parker & Co., proprietors. **Brevoort House** (rates, $1 per day and up), Benjamin & Wentworth, proprietors. **McCoy's New European Hotel** (rates, $1.00 per day and up), Wm. McCoy, proprietor. **Leland Hotel,** Warren F. Leland, proprietor. **Crawford, Maulton, Atlantic.**

CHICOPEE, Mass. Situated on the Connecticut River at the mouth of the Chicopee River. Population, 11,325. *Railroad*—Connecticut River. *Business interests*—Manufacturing.

Hotels—**Cabot House, Chicopee House.**

CHILLICOTHE, Mo. Population, 5885.
Hotels—**Browning House, Markham House, Spencer House, American House.**

CHILLICOTHE, Ohio. Situated on the Scioto River. Population, 10,038. *Railroads*—Marietta & Cincinnati; Scioto Valley—occupy same depot; Dayton & Southeastern. *Business interests*—Agricultural, manufacturing and mercantile.

Hotels—**Emmit House, Warner House.**

CHIPPEWA FALLS, Wis. Situated on the Chippewa River. Population, 4000.
Hotels—**Stanley's, Merchants'.**

CINCINNATI, Ohio. Situated on the Ohio River, opposite the mouth of Licking River. Population, 255,-708. *Railroads*—Cincinnati, Hamilton & Dayton; New

---

This work is circulated gratuitously among prominent hotels of the United States.

LOWRY HOUSE,
HOLLAND, N. Y.

This House is the most conveniently located hotel in town for the traveling public.
 Is first-class in all its appointments and the Commercial Travelers' Home.
 The finest Bar in the country.
 Rooms warmed by an improved Heater. A fine Sample-Room for commercial men.
 The LOWRY HOUSE HALL may be used for Shows and Public Entainments free of charge. Barn and Shed room free.
 Do not let your horses stand out in the street, but drive them in my sheds or barn where it is warm, clean and neat.

TERMS.

Meals, 35 cents. | Lodging, 35 cents.
Two Meals and Lodging, $1.00.

Wagner's Omnibus passes the door and connects with all trains on the B. N. Y. & P. R. R.

C. C. LOWRY, Proprietor.

OPEN ALL NIGHT.

Cor. of Beach Street and Harrison Ave.,
BOSTON, MASS.

BOSTON ❖ HOTEL.

BAXTER & YOUNG, Props.

American and European Plan.

H. C. BAXTER.   WM. A. YOUNG.

Announcement.

New York, June 1st, 1885.

Mr. David Hexter having withdrawn from the management of the **Prescott House**, the undersigned would announce that they have taken charge, and with the change have thoroughly refurnished and renovated the premises, adding a rapid Hydraulic Elevator, running day and night.

The Hotel is located in the business section of the city, and contains one hundred and fifty rooms, at one dollar per day and upwards. The accommodations are the very best, being conducted on the European plan, having annexed a first-class **Restaurant, Lunch Counter** and **Bar**, at reasonable prices, under the control of **Mess. Jahn & Begiebing** (formerly with Hobz & Koennecke).

The **Barber Shop** and **Billiard Room** are newly fitted with the latest improvements and best attendants.

Respectfully,

E. & I. D. HEXTER.

York, Pennsylvania & Ohio—occupy same depot; Ohio & Mississippi; Cincinnati, Washington & Baltimore; Cleveland, Columbus, Cincinnati & Indianapolis; Baltimore and Ohio—occupy same depot; Cincinnati & Portsmouth; Louisville, Cincinnati & Lexington; Pittsburg, Cincinnati & St. Louis—occupy same depot; Toledo; Cincinnati & St Louis—separate depot. Bus transfer for through passengers between depots without change. *Business interests*—Mercantile, manufacturing, commercial, pork packing, &c.

Hotels—**Burnet, St. Clair, St. James, Palace, Hotel Emery, Grand, Gibson, Dennison.**

CIRCLEVILLE, O. Situated on the Scioto River. and Ohio and Erie Canal. Population, 6,000.
Hotels—**The New American, Pickaway House.**

CLARKSVILLE, Tenn. Situated on the Cumberland River. Population, 5010.
Hotels—**Southern, Franklin House, European.**

CLEVELAND, O., second city of the state in size and importance. Situated on Lake Erie, at the mouth of Cuyahoga River. A port of entry. Population, 160,142. *Railroads*—Cleveland, Columbus, Cincinnati & Indianapolis; Cleveland & Pittsburg; Lake Shore & Michigan Southern,—occupy same depot; Atlantic & Great Western,—occupies separate depot;—to which the Cleveland, Columbus, Cincinnati & Indianapolis and Lake Shore & Michigan Southern trains are also run; New York, Chicago & St. Louis,—occupies separate depot. *Business interests*—Commercial, manufacturing and mercantile. It is the northern terminus of the Ohio Canal, connecting Cleveland with the Ohio River at Portsmouth. The

Cuyahoga River affords several miles of dock front, and in its winding course divides the city. The river and valley of the Cuyahoga are spanned, and the two divisions of the city united, by the viaduct, a great structure 2480 feet in length, and costing $2,250,000. Little Mountain, the popular summer resort of the West, is only 20 miles from the city, via Mentor.

Hotels—**Weddell, Kennard, Forest City, American, The Stillman.**

CLINTON. Ia. Situated on the Mississippi River. Population, 9068.

Hotels—**Central House, Revere House.**

CLINTON, Mass. Situated on the Nashua River. Population, 10,000. *Railroads*—Old Colony, Worcester & Nashua, Massachusetts Central,—occupy same depot. *Business interests*—One of the most important manufacturing towns in Worcester County.

Hotel—**Clinton House.**

CLOVERDALE. Cal. Population, 705.

Hotels—**United States, Cloverdale.**

COBOURG, Ont. Situated on Lake Ontario. Population, 5000.

Hotels—**Arlington, Pauwell, Horton House, Windsor, North American, Albion.**

COHOES, N. Y. Situated near the mouth of the Mohawk River, and on the Erie Canal and Champlain Canal. Population, 19,417. *Railroads*—New York Central & Hudson River, Delaware & Hudson Canal Co., (Rensselaer & Saratoga Div.),—occupy separate depots. *Business interests*—Manufacturing (afforded by power which the canal furnishes).

This work is circulated gratuitously among prominent hotels of the United States.

ME**O**MPANY,

E,

TRADE

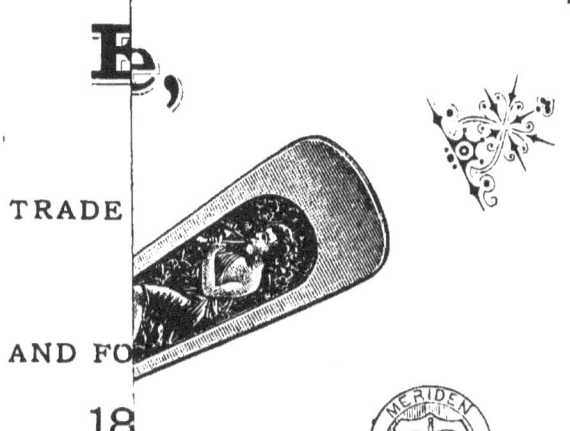

AND FO

18 Trade  Mark

FOR WHITE METAL

W WARE.

OOMS

SQUARE, NEW YORK,
s from Broadway;)

TREET, SAN FRANCISCO,

Main , Hamilton, Ontario.

MERIDEN & BRITANNIA & COMPANY,
Electro Gold & Silver Plate,

TRADE MARK FOR SPOONS, FORKS, ETC.,
"1847 ROGERS BROS., A1"

AND FOR SECTIONAL PLATING,
1847 ROGERS BROS. XII."

Trade　　Mark

FOR WHITE METAL

HOLLOW WARE.

SALESROOMS:
46 EAST 14th STREET, UNION SQUARE, NEW YORK,
(Three doors from Broadway.)
154 STATE STREET, CHICAGO,
134 SUTTER STREET, SAN FRANCISCO,
AND AT THE FACTORIES,

Main Factories, MERIDEN, CONN.　　Branch Factory, Hamilton, Ontario.

Hotels—Harmony, Miller House.

COLLINGWOOD, situated on the Nottawassaga Bay, and inlet of Georgian Bay. Population, 5000.
Hotels—Central, Dominion, True Blue, Manitoba, Globe, Anglo-American.

COLUMBIA, Mo. Population, 3308.
Hotels—Lindell, Southern, Grand Central, Planters', Powers'.

COLUMBIA, S. C. Situated on the Congaree River, at the head of navigation. Population, 10,040. *Railroads*—Greenville & Columbia, South Carolina—occupy same depot; Charlotte, Columbia & Augusta, Wilmington, Columbia & Augusta,—occupy separate depots. *Business interests*—Commercial and mercantile.
Hotels—Columbia, Wright's, Grand Central.

COLUMBIA, Pa. Situated on the Susquehanna River. Population, 8541.
Hotels—Black's, Franklin, American, Continental.

COLUMBIA, Tenn. Situated on the Duck River. Population, 3400.
Hotels—Bethel, Nelson House, Guest House, Depot.

COLUMBUS, Ga. Situated on the Chattahoochee River, opposite Girard, Ala. Population, 12,000. *Railroads*—Mobile & Girard, Central of Georgia (Southwestern Div.), Western of Alabama,—occupy same depot. Columbus & Rome—occupies separate depot. *Business interests*—Manufacturing, cotton and argricultural.
Hotels—Central, Rankin.

COLUMBUS, Miss. Situated on the Tombigbee River. Population, 5350.

For advertising space in this work address the National Directory Co., New York City.

Hotels – **Gilmer, Kennon House, Dowsing House.**

COLUMBUS, Ohio. Situated on the Scioto River. Population, 51,665. *Railroads*—Baltimore & Ohio, Cleveland, Columbus, Cincinnati & Indianapolis, Cleveland, Mt. Vernon & Delaware, Indiana, Bloomington & Western, Columbus, Hocking Valley & Toledo, Pittsburg, Cincinnati & St. Louis, Chicago, St. Louis & Pittsburg, Scioto Valley, Columbus & Sunday Creek Valley,—all roads occupy Union Depot. *Business interests*—Iron, coal, manufacturing and mercantile. Columbus is surrounded by a rich and populous country, and is the center of an active trade.

Hotels— **Park, Neil, United States, American, Corrodi's.**

CONCORD, N. H. Situated on the Merrimack River. Population, 13,838. *Railroads*—Boston, Concord & Montreal; Concord; Concord & Claremont; Northern (N. H)—occupy separate depots. *Business interests*—Manufacturing, mercantile, agricultural and stone quarries.

Hotels—**Phœnix, Elm, Eagle, American House.**

CORINTH, Miss. Population, 2462.
Hotels—**Central, Norris.**

CORNING, N. Y. Situated on the Chemung River, at the terminus of Chemung canal. Population, 4823.
Hotels—**American, Dickinson, Barry, St. James**

CORNWALL, Ont. Situated on the St. Lawrence River. Population, 5000.
Hotels—**St. Lawrence, Central, Commercial, Ottawa House, American House.**

This work is circulated gratuitously among prominent hotels of the United States.

Hotel Washington,

1143 & 1145 WASHINGTON ST.

Opp. Windsor Theatre,   NEW YORK.

EUROPEAN ☦ PLAN

ROOMS BY THE DAY OR WEEK.

HORSE CARS PASS THE DOOR TO AND FROM ALL THE DEPOTS AND THEATRES.

CAFE ⁞ OPEN ⁞ TILL ⁞ MIDNIGHT.

$1.50 PER DAY.

H. M. TEMPLE, Proprietor.

HOTEL ALBERT.
European Plan.

BUILDING ABSOLUTELY FIRE-PROOF

Eleventh Street and University Place, N. Y. City.

GEO. C. WARD.

CORRY, Pa. Population, 5418.
Hotels—St. James, Kent House, Commercial, Phenix.

CORSICANA, Texas. Population, 3500.
Hotels—Malloy House, McKay House, O'Neal House.

COSHOCTON, O. Situated at the confluence of the Walhonding and Tuscarawas rivers. Population, 3044.
Hotels—Park Hotel, McDonald, Price, Central.

COUNCIL BLUFFS, Iowa. Situated at the foot of high bluffs overlooking a level plain which stretches to the Missouri River, about three miles distant. Population, 18,059. Council Bluffs is the western terminus of the Chicago & Northwestern, Chicago, Rock Island & Pacific, Chicago, Burlington & Quincy, and Chicago, Milwaukee & St. Paul Railroads, the four trunk lines from the East, as well as of the Kansas City, St. Joseph & Council Bluffs, Wabash, St. Louis & Pacific, Union Pacific, and Sioux City & Pacific Railroads, all of which have independent stations in the town and occupy the Union Pacific depot (a mile nearer the river) in common. *Business interests*—Mercantile.
Hotels—Union Pacific, Ogden House, Pacific House.

COVINGTON, Ky. Situated on the Ohio River, opposite Cincinnati, Ohio, with which it is connected by suspension bridge, street railways and steam ferry. It is also connected with Newport by suspension bridge. Population, 29,720. *Railroads*—Louisville, Cincinnati & Lexington; Kentucky Central occupy separate depots. *Business interests*—Manufacturing and mercantile.
Hotels—Clinton, National, Ashbrook, Central.

For advertising space in this work address the National Directory Co., New York City.

CRAWFORDSVILLE, Ind. Population, 5000.
Hotels—**St. James, Sherman House, Nutt's.**

CRESCO, Iowa. Population. 1875.
Hotels—**Dillworth, Strother, Mason, Van Slyke.**

CRESTON, Iowa. Population, 5116.
Hotels—**Creston, Commercial, Metropolitan, Summit, Revere.**

CUMBERLAND, Md. Situated on the Potomac River. It is also the western terminus of the Chesapeake and Ohio Canal. Population, 10,666. *Railroads* —Baltimore & Ohio; Cumberland & Pennsylvania; Pennsylvania (Bedford Division)—occupy same depot. *Business interests*—Coal trade and manufacturing.
Hotels—**Queen City, St. Nicholas, City, Washington.**

DALLAS, Texas. Situated on the Trinity River. Population. 10,358. *Railroads*—Missouri Pacific (Dallas Extension); Houston & Texas Central; Texas & Pacific; Chicago, Texas & Mexican Central; Texas Trunk, occupy separate depots. *Business interests*—Mercantile, agricultural and manufacturing.
Hotels—**Grand Windsor, St. George, National.**

DALTON. Ga. Population, 2560.
Hotels—**National. Exchange, Rudd House.**

DANBURY, Ct. Situated on the Still River. Population. 11,660. *Railroads*—Danbury & Norwalk; Housatonic; New York & New England, occupy separate depots. *Business interests*—Hat manufacturing.
Hotels—**Wooster House, Turner House.**

DANVERS, Mass. Population, 6500.
Hotels—**Danver's, Central House.**

This work is circulated gratuitously among prominent hotels of the United States.

Hotel Shelburn

Fifth Ave. and 36th St.

New York

⊲BLINN BROTHERS⊳

Formerly of HOTEL BRUNSWICK.

GEDNEY HOUSE,

40th Street and Broadway,

NEW YORK

EUROPEAN ✦ PLAN

Rooms $1.00 per Day and Upward.

◁ FIRST-CLASS IN EVERY RESPECT ▷

BOWERS BROS., Props.

DANVILLE, Ill. Situated at the forks of the Big Vermillion River. Population, 7751.
Hotels—Ætna House, St. James, Arlington, Tremont House, Sherman House.

DANVILLE, Pa. Population, 7934.
Hotels—Montour, City, Danville House.

DANVILLE, Ky. Population, 3090.
Hotels—Central, Gilcher's, Clemens.

DANVILLE, Va. Situated on the Dan River. Population, 7536.
Hotels—Arlington, Hancock, Windsor.

DAVENPORT, Iowa. Situated on the Mississippi River, opposite Rock Island, Ill. Population, 21,834. *Railroads*—Chicago, Rock Island & Pacific; Chicago, Milwaukee & St. Paul, occupy separate depots. *Business interests*—Agricultural, mercantile and manufacturing.
Hotels—Kimball House, St. James, Newcomb, Ackly.

DAYTON, O. Situated at the confluence of the Mad and Miami Rivers, and on the Miami Canal. Population, 38,677. *Railroads*—New York, Pennsylvania & Ohio; Cincinnati, Hamilton & Dayton; Cleveland, Columbus, Cincinnati & Indianapolis; Dayton & Union; Pittsburg, Cincinnati & St. Louis; Dayton & Southeastern, occupy same depot. *Business interests*—Manufacturing, mercantile and agricultural.
Hotels—Beckel, Phillips', Merchants', Schieble.

DECATUR, Ill. Situated on the Sangamon River. Population, 9449.

For advertising space in this work address the National Directory Co., New York City.

Hotels - **St. Nicholas** ($2 per day), **New Deming Palace, Central House.**

DEDHAM, Mass. Population, 6202.
Hotel **Phœnix.**

DEFIANCE, Ohio. Population 5911.
Hotels —**Crosby, Empire, Russell, American, Central.**

DELAWARE, Ohio. Population, 7000.
Hotels —**American, Central, Powell.**

DELPHOS, Ohio. Located on the Miami and Erie Canal. Population, 3814.
Hotels —**Brown's, St. Charles, Delphos, Hoehn's, Mansion, Phelan, Rose.**

DENISON, Tex. Population, 4500.
Hotels —**Planters', Lamar, Cameron, White House.**

DENVER, Col. Capital. Situated at the confluence of Cherry Creek and the South Platte River. Population 35,630. *Railroads* —Kansas Div., Colorado Div., Denver & South Park Div., and Boulder Branch of the Union Pacific Railroad ; Denver & Rio Grande ; Denver & New Orleans ; Chicago, Burlington & Quincy, Colorado Div. Denver is fourteen miles from the foot hills, and from her streets are seen more than 300 miles of the Rocky Mountains. Denver's volume of business in 1870 (exclusive of banks) was $37,551,593. Colorado Mines reached from here produced in bullion not less than $22,000,000 annually ; and the other products of the State, live stock, &c., exceed $5,000,000.

Hotels —**Windsor, St. James, American** ($2.50 and $3 per day), **Charpiot's, Tremont, Alvord, Brunswick, Lindell.**

This work is circulated gratuitously among prominent hotels of the United States.

St. Nicholas Hotel

Fronting Broadway, Washington Place and Mercer St.

NEW YORK CITY.

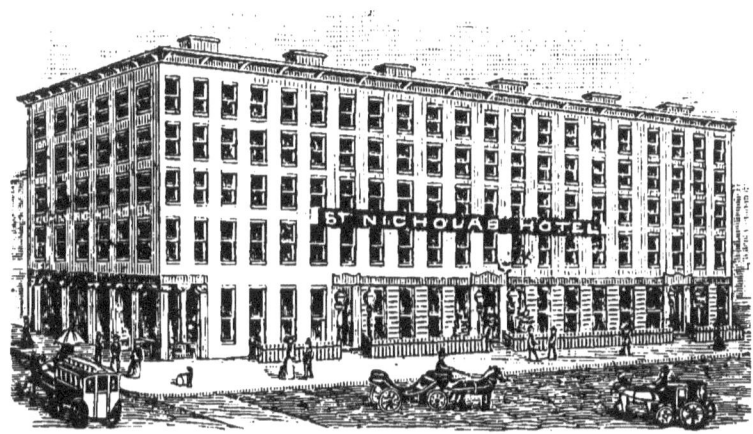

Superior Accommodations for 300 Guests.

Most Desirable Location in the city for Business and Pleasure Parties; within easy access of all the Ferries, Depots, Places of Amusement and Points of Interest. Distant from Cooper Union, Astor Library and Washington Square 100 yards, and only 500 yards below Union Square. Excellent Restaurant, Dining Hall, Cafe, Chess, Billiard, Tonsorial and Reading Parlors, with One Hundred Daily and Weekly Papers on File.

European Plan, - - - $1 per day and upward.
American Plan, - - - $2.50 per day and upward.

The undersigned assures all who may favor him with their patronage that neither pains nor expense will be spared on his part to make them comfortable at the most economical rates.

JULIUS A. ROBINSON, *Owner and Manager.*

Golden Hill Hotel

◄ 19, 21 & 23 ►

HARRISON AVENUE,

Bridgeport, Conn.

$1.50 TO $1.75 PER DAY.

Special Rates by the Week.

DE PERE, Wis. Population, 4000.
Hotels—**Commercial House, Transit House.**

DES MOINES, Iowa. Capital. Situated at the confluence of the Des Moines and Raccoon Rivers. Population, 22,408. The State House and offices are on the east, while the larger portion of the city is on the west side of the Des Moines River. The United States Court House and a Baptist college are also located here. *Railroads*—Chicago, Rock Island & Pacific; Des Moines & Fort Dodge; Chicago & Northwestern; Wabash, St. Louis & Pacific; Des Moines Northwestern; St. Louis, Des Moines & Northern; Chicago, Burlington & Quincy; Des Moines, Osceola & Southern—all roads occupy separate depots. *Business interests*—Mercantile, coal, manufacturing and agricultural.
Hotels—**Aborn, Kirkwood, Capital City, Sabin, Gault, Morgan.**

DE SOTO, Mo. Situated forty-two miles south of St. Louis. Population, 1989.
Hotels—**De Soto Jefferson, Turley, European.**

DETROIT, Mich. Situated on the Detroit River, seven miles below Lake St. Clair, and eighteen miles above Lake Erie. Population, 116,342. *Railroads*—Canada Southern; Detroit & Bay City; Detroit, Lansing & Northern; Lake Shore & Michigan Southern; Michigan Central; Great Western of Canada—occupy same depot; Detroit, Grand Haven & Milwaukee, and Grand Trunk —occupy same depot. *Business interests*—Commercial, mercantile and manufacturing.
Hotels—**Russell** ($2.50, $3 and $3.50 per day), **Gris-**

For advertising space in this work address the National Directory Co., New York City.

wold ($2 and $2.50 per day), **Michigan Exchange, Brunswick, Cass, Franklin, Rice's, Tremont.**

DETROIT, Minn. Situated on the line of the Northern Pacific Railroad and banks of the Detroit Lake.
Hotels—**Lake Side, American, Wilson, Detroit, Northwestern.**

DIXON, Ill. Situated on the Rock River, about seventy miles above the Mississippi. Population, 4242.
Hotel—**Waverly.**

DOVER, N. H. Situated on the Cocheco River, at the head of sloop navigation. Population, 11,687. *Railroads*—Boston & Maine; Eastern—occupy separate depots. *Business interests*, Manufacturing and commercial.
Hotels—**American, Kimball, New Hampshire House.**

DUBUQUE, Iowa. Situated on the west bank of the Mississippi River, 470 miles above St. Louis, and 321 miles below St. Paul, at an elevation of 576 feet above the Gulf of Mexico. Population, 22,254. *Railroads*—Chicago, Milwaukee & St. Paul; Illinois Central—occupy separate depots. *Business interests*, Manufacturing and mercantile, mining, lumber, &c.
Hotels—**Julien House, Lorimier House** ($2 and $2.50 per day), **Key City House.**

DULUTH, Minn. Situated at the head of Lake Superior. Population, 3483.
Hotels—**Bay View House, St. Louis, Windsor, Wakelin.**

DUNKIRK, N. Y. Population, 6900.
Hotels—**Commercial, Eastern, Erie.**

This work is circulated gratuitously among prominent hotels of the United States.

SEASON 1885.

Long Beach Hotel,
LONG BEACH, LONG ISLAND.

Take Ferry foot of East 34th St.

THE charming climate of LONG BEACH, its cool breezes, the absence of mosquitoes and the ordinary plagues of summer watering places, its easy accessibility to New York, and the class of people that has already contributed to its character—all these have established it as the

First of all Resorts on the Atlantic Coast.

The natural conditions, the toppgraphy of the Beach and the tidal flow, has made the location without a rival in a sanitary point of view. The climate is a specific for hay fever, and for all such stubborn ailments.

It is now conceded that there is no such bathing beach anywhere on the sea coast as at LONG BEACH. We are pleased to announce to the children that the inlet for still-water bathing is forming for the season of 1885. The fishing for the last two seasons has been better here than at any other point on the Long Island coast. Boats for rowing, sailing and blue fishing will be provided; and all the diversions for which the south side of Long Island is celebrated will be enjoyed this summer in the fullest degree by the guests at the LONG BEACH HOTEL.

The best Musical Talent has been engaged.

Frequent and Fast Trains, through from Hunter's Point and Brooklyn, will be run by the Long Island Railroad, making the time to the Beach in forty-five minutes, with no change of cars.

Special Rates for Families. Prices to suit the times.

SOUTHGATE, MURRAY & WILKINSON,
Proprietors.

Albemarle Hotel

NEW YORK.

*MOST CHARMINGLY AND MOST CEN-
TRALLY SITUATED.*

Junction of Broadway, Fifth Ave. and 24th St.,

FACING MADISON SQUARE.

Conducted on the European Plan.

JAUVIN & WALTER, Props.

EASTMAN, Ga. The town is situated about 700 feet above tide-water, in the midst of the pine forests of Georgia. Population, 500.
Hotels—**Uplands, Railroad House.**

EASTON, Pa. Situated on the Delaware River, above the mouth of the Lehigh River; also, located at Junction of the Delaware, and Lehigh and Morris Canals. Population, including South Easton, 11,924. *Railroads*—Central of New Jersey—occupies separate depot; Delaware, Lackawanna & Western; Lehigh Valley—occupy same depot. *Business interests*—Iron and its manufacture.
Hotels—**United States, Franklin House.**

EAST SAGINAW, Mich. Situated on the east bank of the Saginaw River, twenty miles from its mouth, and the head of Saginaw Bay. Population, 19,016. *Railroads* —Flint & Pere Marquette; Saginaw, Tuscola & Huron; Port Huron & North-western, occupy same depot; Michigan Central; Detroit & Bay City, occupy same depot. *Business interests*—The center of the largest lumber and salt district in the United States.
Hotels—**Bancroft, Everett, Sherman, Lloyd, American, Neagley.**

EAST ST. LOUIS, Ill. Situated on the Mississippi River, opposite St. Louis, Mo. Population, 10,000. *Railroads*—Cairo & St. Louis; Chicago & Alton; Chicago, Burlington & Quincy; Illinois & St. Louis; Indianapolis & St. Louis; Ohio & Mississippi; St. Louis, Vandalia, Terra Haute & Indianapolis; St. Louis, Alton & Terra Haute; Louisville & Nashville; Wabash, St. Louis & Pacific, centre at Relay Depot; Toledo, Cincinnati & St. Louis, occupies separate depot. *Business interests*—

For advertising space in this work address the National Directory Co., New York City.

Manufacturing, elevator business and St. Louis National Stock Yards. The great steel bridge connects East St. Louis with St. Louis.
Hotel—**Martell.**

EAU CLAIRE, Wis. Situated on the Chippewa River at the mouth of the Eau Claire River. Population, 10,118. *Railroads*—Chicago, St. Paul, Minneapolis and Omaha line (Eastern Div.); Chippewa Falls & Western; Wisconsin Central—occupy same depot; Chicago, Milwaukee & St. Paul—separate depot. *Business interests*—Lumber and flouring mills. Eau Claire lumber mills cut and ship upwards of 50,000,000 feet of pine lumber annually.
Hotels- **Eau Claire House, Galloway House.**

EDGEFIELD, Tenn. Situated on the Cumberland River, opposite Nashville. Population, 4380.
Hotel—**Edgefield.**

ELGIN, Ill. Situated on both sides of the Fox River, and called East and West Elgin. Population, 10,040. *Railroads*—Chicago, Milwaukee & St. Paul; Chicago & Northwestern—occupy separate depots. *Business interests*—Manufacturing, mercantile, agricultural, &c. Among the manufactures of Elgin is the National (Elgin) Watch Factory.
Hotels—**Nolting House, Central, Kimball, Jennings', Commercial, New Windsor.**

ELIZABETH, N. J. Population, 28,229. *Railroads*—Central of New Jersey; Pennsylvania (New York Div.). occupy same depot. *Business interests*—Shipment of coal and manufacturing. The city is situated on elevated

---

This work is circulated gratuitously among prominent hotels of the United States.

United States Hotel

ON THE EUROPEAN PLAN.

Fulton, Water and Pearl Sts., N. Y.

J. L. TRUMAN, Proprietor.

SINGLE ROOMS, 50 cents to $1.50.
        DOUBLE ROOMS, $1.50 to $3.00

New York Elevated Railroad Depot in the Hotel. Time to Grand Central Depot, 30 minutes. Five minutes' walk to New Haven, Hartford and Bridgeport steamers.

AM RICAN PLAN.— Full Board, $2.50, $3.00 to $3.50 per day.
ROOMS (on European Plan)—$1.00 per day and upwards.

Special Rates for Families and Permanent Guests.

KEEFERS

GRAND CENTRAL HOTEL,
667 TO 677 BROADWAY.

THIS Hotel is within one block of four lines of Street and Elevated Railroads. Three lines of Stages pass the door, affording rapid communication with business centres and places of Amusement, and is justly regarded as the best Family Hotel in the City.

ground, is regularly laid out with broad, straight streets. finely shaded and crossing each other at right angles.
Hotels—Sheridan, Schwartz, City, Shreve's.

ELIZABETHTOWN, Ky. Population, 3500.
Hotels—'hower's House, Hill's.

ELKHART, Ind. Situated at the confluence of St. Joseph and Elkhart Rivers. Population, 6939.
Hotels—Clifton House, Elkhart House.

ELMIRA, N. Y. Population, 20,541. *Railroads*—New York, Lake Erie & Western; Northern Central; Tioga & Elmira State Line—occupy Union depot; Utica, Ithaca & Elmira; New York, Lackawanna & Western—occupy same depot. *Business interests*—Manufacturing and mercantile.
Hotels—Rathbun House, Frazier House ($2 per day), Delavan House.

EL PASO, Texas. Situated on east bank of the Rio Grande River, near the northwest corner of the State. Population, 736.
Hotels—Central, Rinson, American, Pacific.

ELYRIA, Ohio. Situated at the confluence of the two branches of Black River. Population, 5000.
Hotels—Metropolitan, Beebe, American, National.

EMPORIA, Kan. Situated between Cottonwood and Neosho Rivers, and about one mile from either. Population, 4868.
Hotels—Windsor, Merchants'.

- ERIE, Pa. Situated on Lake Erie. A port of entry. Population, 27,730. The harbor, one of the best and largest on the lake, is an important place of outfit for

For advertising space in this work address the National Directory Co., New York City.

vessels, and remarkable for its flourishing trade. *Railroads*—Erie & Pittsburg ; Lake Shore & Michigan Southern ; Pennsylvania (Philadelphia & Erie Div.) occupy same depot ; New York, Chicago & St. Louis- separate depot. *Business interests*—Manufacturing, lake commerce and fisheries.

Hotels—**Union Depot, Morton House, Ellsworth House, Reed House** ; also, **Massassauqua Point Hotel**, at head of bay, a summer resort.

EUFAULA, Ala. Situated on the Chattahoochee River. Population. 3875.

Hotels—**Central, Stubblefield, National, Finnerty House.**

EUREKA SPRINGS, Ark. Terminus of the Eureka Springs Railway, and nineteen miles from Seligman, on the St. Louis & San Francisco Railway. Population, 5000.

Hotels—**Perry House, Southern, Hancock.**

EVANSTON, Ill. Situated on Lake Michigan, twelve miles north of Chicago. Population, 4820.

Hotels—**Avenue, French's, Lakeside.**

EVANSVILLE, Ind. Situated on the Ohio River. Population, 29,280. (Location of the Uni ed States Marine Hospital, 192 miles above Cairo, 175 miles below Louisville). *Railroads*—Evansville & Terre Haute; Louisville, Evansville & St. Louis occupy same depot ; Evansville & Nashville ; St. Louis & Evansville Div. of Louisville & Nashville - occupy same depot ; Peoria, Decatur & Evansville -- separate depot. Passengers in through cars transferred to and from depots of Evansville & Terre Haute and Louisville & Nashville (Evansville,

This work is circulated gratuitously among prominent hotels of the United States.

HOFFMAN HOUSE
BROADWAY AND MADISON SQUARE, - - NEW YORK.

—A—
FAVORITE
FAMILY
HOTEL

HOTEL
NEWLY
FURNISHED
Throughout.

Restaurant, Cafe and Salons unexcelled. | Rooms, $2.00 per Day and Upwards.

C. H. READ & CO., Proprietors.

COLEMAN HOUSE,   ERIE RAILWAY DINING HALL,
BROADWAY AND 27TH STREET, N Y.   HORNELLSVILLE, N. Y.
JAS. H. RODGERS,   JAS. H. RODGERS, Prop.
PROPRIETOR.   WM. A. RODGERS, Mangr.

The Kensington

Saratoga Springs, N. Y.

THE above-named Hotel, which has grown so rapidly in favor, and is acknowledged to have the most pleasant and healthy location in Saratoga, will commence its fourth season Saturday, June 13th, with greatly increased facilities and very promising prospects.

During the winter it has been improved by an addition of a hundred elegant rooms, many of them en suite, with Bath and Toilet attached; a Gentlemen's Reading Room, Billiard Room, Play-room for children, new Dining-Room and new Kitchen, in which are Driven Wells, supplying the purest water. The Parlor has been handsomely decorated, and the power and speed of the Elevator increased.

The Table will be second to none in the country, and Franko's Celebrated Parlor Orchestra will furnish first-class music.

Apply at the Coleman House, N. Y., until June 1st, 1885.

JAS. H. RODGERS,
Owner and Proprietor.

Henderson & Nashville Div.), without change, *Business interests*—Commercial, manufacturing, mercantile, coal, &c.
Hotels—St. George, Sherwood, St. Cloud, Hedderich, Farmers', Williams'.

FALL RIVER, Mass. Situated on Mount Hope Bay, at mouth of the Taunton River. Population, 49,006. *Railroads*—Old Colony; Fall River—occupy same depot; Fall River Railroad to New Bedford in separate depot. *Business interests*—Manufacturing cotton and iron works.
Hotels— **Narragansett, Wilbour's, Lagrange, Thurston.**

FARGO, Dakota Ter. Situated in the famous Red River Valley, and on the extreme eastern boundary of the Territory.
Hotels—**Continental, Headquarters, Sherman.**

FARIBAULT, Minn. Population, 5428.
Hotels—**Arlington, Ogden, U. S. Hotel.**

FAYETTEVILLE, Tenn. Population, 2150.
Hotels—**McElroy House, Petty House.**

FERGUS FALLS, Minn. At the great rapids of the Red River of the North. Population, Dec. 1, 1881, 2954.
Hotels—**Bell's, Occidental.**

FERNANDINA, Fla. Situated on the northern part of Amelia Island, 185 miles east of Tallahassee, and 27 miles north of Jacksonville. Population, 2026.
Hotels—**Mansion, Egmont, Florida Dell and Strathmore on Fernandina Beach.**

FINDLAY, O. Population, 4846.
Hotels—**Joy, Commercial, Sherman House.**

For advertising space in this work address the National Directory Co., New York City.

FITCHBURG, Mass. Population, 12,405. *Railroads*—Chesire; Fitchburg; Old Colony—all roads occupy same depot. *Business interests*—Manufacturing and Mercantile.
Hotels Fitchburg, American.

FLINT, Mich. Situated on the Flint River. Population, 8418.
Hotels Bryant, Sherman, Dayton, Thayer, Mason, Waverly.

FOND DU LAC, Wis. Situated at foot of Lake Winnebago, and at the mouth of a river of the same name. Population, 13,091. *Railroads* Chicago & Northwestern; Fond du Lac, Amboy & Peoria; Wisconsin Central—occupy separate depots. *Business interests* Mercantile, manufacturing, iron, lumber, &c.
Hotel American. ($2.00 per day).

FORT DODGE, Ia. Population, 3700.
Hotels Duncombe House, St. Charles, Patoson, Fort Dodge House.

FORT EDWARD, N. Y. Situated on the Hudson River; also, on Champlain Canal. Population, 3498.
Hotels St. James, Eldridge, Milliman.

FORT MADISON, Ia. Situated on the Mississippi River. Population, 4678
Hotels Metropolitan, Central, Kasten, Madison.

FORT SCOTT, Kan. Population, 5512.
Hotels Wilder House, Gulf House, Lockwocd House, German House.

FORT WAYNE, Ind. Situated at the confluence of the St. Joseph's and St. Mary's Rivers, which, united

---

This work is circulated gratuitously among prominent hotels of the United States.

UNION HOUSE
UNION STREET,
Opposite City Market, - - NEW HAVEN, CONN.

$2.00 per Day.

R. T. CHADBOURNE, Prop.

THIS HOUSE HAS BEEN NEW-RIGGED THROUGHOUT.

GRAND UNION HOTEL,
1016 CHAPEL STREET,
Opposite Colleges, NEW HAVEN, CONN.

The best appointed, only modern House in the city, and one of the most popular in New England. Large, pleasant rooms. All have steam heat, gas, electric bells, hot and cold water. Table and service first-class. Elegant Bar and Billiard Room connected.

$3.00 a Day. Discount to Commercial Travelers.

SOUTHWICK & CO., - - Proprietors.

STERLNG HOUSE,
Bridgeport, Conn.

FRANK H. WHITING, Prop'r.

RATES.—Per day, $2.00; ¾ day, $1.75; ½ day, $1.25.

DISCOUNT BY THE WEEK.

BATH HOTEL
BATH, MAINE.

Close to the Kenebec River.

Band Concerts and Art Parlors free.

Transient, - - $2.00 per Day.

Rooms for twenty more Summer Boarders at $10 and less per week.

MELLEN PLUMMER, Proprietor.

CENTRAL HOUSE

Salem, Washington Co., N. Y.

B. G. RICE, - - **Proprietor.**

This is a First-Class Summer Resort.

Several Lakes are in the neighborhood, with good Fishing, Bathing and Boating, and

THE DRIVES ARE UNEXCELLED.

form the Maumee River. Population, 26,880. *Railroads* —Fort Wayne & Jackson; Fort Wayne, Muncie & Cincinnati—occupy same depot; Grand Rapids & Indiana; Pittsburg, Fort Wayne & Chicago; Wabash, St. Louis & Pacific—occupy same depot. *Business interests*—Here are located the locomotive works, car and repair shops of the Pittsburg, Fort Wayne & Chicago Railway, which, with the general offices of the western division of the same railway, occupy a square of some five acres in extent. The largest manufactures are in lumber, woolen mills, plaining mills, foundries, wagons, carriages, etc.

Hotels—**Aveline, Mayer's, Robinson House.**

FORT WORTH. Tex. 253 miles S. W. of Texarkana. Population, 7000.

Hotels—**El Paso, Waterman's.**

FRAMINGHAM, Mass. Population, 5729.

Hotel—**Framingham.**

FRANKFORT, Ky. Situated on the Kentucky River, sixty miles from its mouth. Population, 6979.

Hotels—**Capital, Merriwether's.**

FRANKLIN, Pa. Situated on the Allegheny River. Population, 5500.

Hotels—**United States, Exchange, Rural, National, Grant House.**

FREDERICK, Md. Situated near the Monocacy River. Population, 8486.

Hotels—**City, Groff, Carlin House.**

FREDERICKSBURG, Va. Situated on the Rappahannock River. Population, 5000.

Hotels—**Central, Exchange.**

For advertising space in this work address the National Directory Co., New York City.

FREDERICTON. N. B. Situated on the River St. John. Population. 7000.
Hotels—Queen, Barker, Bayley, Long's, Waverly, Commercial.

FREDERICKTOWN. Mo. 104 miles south of St. Louis. Population, 1805.
Hotels—Madison, White, Allen.

FREEHOLD. N. J. Population, 3000.
Hotels—American. Union, Washington and Railroad House.

FREEPORT, Ill. Population, 10,000. *Railroads*—Chicago & Northwestern; Illinois Central; Chicago, Milwaukee & St. Paul (Racine & Southwestern Div.),—occupy separate depots. *Business interests*—Manufacturing and agricultural.
Hotels—Brewster, Clifton, Pennsylvania.

FREMONT, O. Situated on the Sandusky River. at the head of navigation. Population, 8496.
Hotels—Ball House, Tell House.

FROSTBURG, Md. Population. 6000.
Hotels—St. Cloud, Grand Central.

FULTON, N. Y. Situated on the Oswego River. Population. 4648.
Hotels— Johnson House, Fulton House, Lewis House.

GALENA. Ill. Situated on the Galena River. Population, 8200.
Hotels—De Soto House, European, Mississippi, Lawrence.

GALESBURG, Ill. Population. 11,446. Seat of

This work is circulated gratuitously among prominent hotels of the United States.

Lombard University and Knox College and Seminary. Engine houses, machine and repair shops of Middle Division of Chicago, Burlington & Quincy Railroad located here. *Railroad*—Chicago, Burlington & Quincy, Main Line, and Peoria and Quincy Divisions. *Business interests*—Manufacturing and mercantile ; centre of broomcorn district.

Hotels—**Union, Brown's** ($2 per day).

GALLATIN, Tenn. Population, 4000.
Hotels—**Sindle House, Sumner.**

GALT, Ont. Population, 5000.
Hotels—**Queen's, Central.**

GALVESTON, Tex. Located on an island between the Gulf of Mexico and Galveston Bay. A port of entry. Population, 22,253. *Railroads*—Galveston, Houston & Henderson ; Gulf, Colorado & Santa Fé—occupy Union depot. *Business interests*—Mercantile and commercial.

Hotels—**Tremont, Girard'n, Washington.**

GENEVA, N. Y. Situated at the head of Seneca Lake. Population, 5861.
Hotels—**Franklin, American, International.**

GETTYSBURG, Pa. Population, 3114.
Hotels—**Spring. Eagle, McClellan, Keystone, Washington, Globe, Battle Field.**

GLOUCESTER, Mass. Situated on Cape Ann. Peninsula projecting into the Atlantic Ocean, forming the north limit of Massachusetts Bay, and the south limit of Ipswich Bay. Comprises Lanesville, Bay View, Annisquam, and West Gloucester on Ipswich Bay, and East Gloucester, Gloucester (harbor), and Magnolia on

For advertising space in this work address the National Directory Co., New York City.

Massachusetts Bay. Population, 19,329. *Railroad*—Eastern (Gloucester branch). *Business interests*—Massachusetts Bay side, fisheries; Ipswich Bay side, granite.

Hotels **Pavilion, Ocean, Atlantic, Webster, Belmont.** *Summer houses*—**Pavilion, Bass Rocks, Pebbly Beach.** At East Gloucester: **Craig Cottage, Delphine.** At Magnolia: **Willow Cottage, Hesperus, Ocean Side, Oak Grove.** At Annisquam: **Highland House.**

GLOVERSVILLE, N. Y. Population, 7400.
Hotels—**Mason, Alvord, Scoville.**

GOLDSBORO, N. C. Population, 3415.
Hotels—**Humphrey, Bonitz.**

GRAND FORKS, Dak. Situated on the Red River, in the richest wheat-growing region in the Northwest. Population, 1703.

Hotels—**Griggs, Mansard, Northwestern.**

GRAND HAVEN, Mich. Situated on Lake Michigan, at the mouth of Grand River. Population, 4862.

Hotels—**Cutler House, Kirby House.**

GRAND RAPIDS, Mich. Situated on Grand River. Population, 32,015. *Railroads*—Chicago & West Michigan; Grand Rapids & Indiana; Michigan Central—occupy same depot; Detroit, Grand Haven & Milwaukee; Grand Rapids, Newaygo & Lake Shore; Lake Shore & Michigan Southern occupy separate depots. *Business interests*—Manufacturing, commercial, lumber, &c.

Hotels—**Sweet's**, (rates, $2.50, $3.00, $3.50 per day.) **Morton, Rathbun, Bridge Street, Eagle.**

GREAT FALLS, N. H. Situated on the Salmon Falls River. Population, 8000.

This work is circulated gratuitously among prominent hotels of the United States.

HOTEL NUMA

20 & 22 Hayward Place,

Near Globe Theatre. **BOSTON, MASS.**

PRIVATE DINING ROOMS.

Steaks, Chops, and Fish a Specialty.

FRANK N. MAINE, Prop.

FREEMAN & HOUSE

(FORMERLY ADAMS HOUSE),

46 & 48 Union Street, Providence, R. I.

Three Minutes Walk from Gen'l Passenger Depot.

FREEMAN & WEEKS, Proprs.

$1.50 and $2.00 per Day.

Special Rates to the Theatrical Profession and Commercial Travelers.
First-Class Sample and Billiard Rooms.
Bath-Rooms free to Patrons.

Elm House,

36 John St.

(6 doors fr. Main)

Bridgeport, Ct.

Seventy-five Rooms Heated by Steam, entirely Remodeled and Newly Furnished.

J. R. Rockfeller,
PROPRIETOR.

Board by the Day or Week.

$1.50 per Day.

Liberal Discount.

Hotels- Great Falls, Grant's, Granite State.

GREEN BAY, Wis. Situated at the head of Green Bay and mouth of Fox River. Population, 7479.
Hotels- Cook's and American.

GREEN LAKE, Wis. Post office—DARTFORD, Green Lake Co., Wis.
Hotels—Hill's, Sherwood Forest, Oakwood House, Pleasant Point House.

GREENBUSH, N. Y. Situated on the Hudson River, opposite Albany, N. Y. Connected with Albany by two iron railroad bridges and one new team and railroad bridge. Population, 5021.
Hotels—Rensselaer, Boston, Broadway.

GREENCASTLE, Ind. Population, 3611.
Hotels— Central, Jones'.

GREENSBORO, N. C. Population, 4996.
Hotels—Central, McAdoo House, Benbow House,. Planters.

GREENSBORO, Ala. Population, 1850.
Hotel—Cowin House.

GREENSBURG, Pa. Population, 3300.
Hotels—Dixon House, Laird House, Miller House, Zimmerman House.

GREENVILLE, Ala. Population, 2500.
Hotels—Perry, Mallett Marion.

GREENVILLE, Pa. Situated on the Shenango Creek, a tributary of the Beaver River; also, on Erie Canal. Population, 4601.
Hotels—National, Fell House, Packard House.

GREENVILLE, S. C. Situated on the Reedy River. Population, 6155.
Hotels—**Central, Commercial, Exchange, Greenville, Mansion House.**

GREENWICH, Ct. Situated on Long Island Sound. Population, 7965.
Hotels—**Morton House, Lenox House.**

GRENADA. Miss. Situated on the Yellow Busha, navigable four months in the year. Population, 2460.
Hotels—**Chamberlin (at depot), Walthall.**

GRIFFIN, Ga. Population, 4200.
Hotels—**Nelm's House, Wheeler House, Goddard House.**

GUELPH, Ont. Situated on the Speed River. Population, 11,000. *Railroads*—Grand Trunk, Great Western of Canada,—occupy separate depots. *Business interests*—Manufacturing, mercantile and argricultural.
Hotels—**American, Dominion, Queen's, Royal, Wellington, Western, &c.**

HACKENSACK, N. J. Situated on the Hackensack River. Population, 4500.
Hotels—**National, Washington, Hackensack, Mansion**

HAGERSTOWN. Md. Population, 7098.
Hotels—**Baldwin, Franklin, Antietam, City.**

HALIFAX. Capital of Nova Scotia. Situated on an inlet of the Atlantic Ocean, called Halifax Harbor. Population, 30,000. *Railroad*—Intercolonial. *Business interests*—Manufacturing, commercial, shipping. Halifax is the principal commercial and naval station of the North

This work is circulated gratuitously among prominent hotels of the United States.

HOWLAND HOTEL,

LONG BRANCH, N. J.

American Plan. Open June to September.

N. B. BARRY, Proprietor.

GLENHAM HOTEL

FIFTH AVENUE,

Between 21st & 22d Streets, near Madison Square,

NEW YORK.

EUROPEAN PLAN

N. B. BARRY, Proprietor.

Hotel ※ St. ※ Stephen

EUROPEAN PLAN

42 to 52 EAST ELEVENTH ST.

Bet. Broadway and University Place,

New York

W. D. RYDER, Proprietor

Single Rooms, $1.00 per Day and Upward.

Double Rooms, $2.00 per Day and Upward.

American Colonies, and its harbor is one of the best known.
Hotels—**Halifax, International, Carlton, Waverly, Royal.**

HAMILTON, O. Situated on the Miami River and Miami and Erie Canal. Population, 12,122. *Railroad*—Cincinnati, Hamilton & Dayton. *Business interests*—Mercantile, manufacturing and agricultural.
Hotels—**Phillips, Straub, St. James.**

HAMILTON, Ont. Situated an Burlington Bay. Population, 34,000. *Railroads*—Great Western of Canada; Wellington, Grey & Bruce—occupy same depot; Hamilton & Northwestern—separate depot. *Business interests* - Manufacturing, mercantile, agricultural.
Hotels—**Royal, St. Nicholas, Dominion, American, Lee's, Mansion House, Walker House.**

HANNIBAL, Mo. Situated on the Mississippi River. Population, 11,074. *Railroads*—Chicago, Burlington & Quincy; Missouri Pacific (Missouri, Kansas & Texas Div.); St. Louis, Keokuk & Northwestern; St. Louis, Hannibal & Keokuk; Wabash, St. Louis & Pacific; Hannibal & St. Joseph— all occupy Union depot *Business interests*—Lumber, lime. oil, salt beef and pork packing, &c.
Hotels—**Park, Planters, Continental, Union Depot.**

HANOVER, Pa. Population, 2317.
Hotels—**Central, Diller, Franklin, American.**

HARRISBURG, Pa. Capital. Situated on the Susquehanna River. Population, 30,762. *Railroads*—Cumberland Valley; Northern Central; Pennsylvania- occupy same depot; Philadelphia & Reading; Schuylkill &

For advertising space in this work address the National Directory Co., New York City.

Susquehanna - occupy separate depots. *Business interests* —principally iron manufactories.
Hotels—**Lochiel, Bolton, United States, Jones.**

HARTFORD. Conn. Capital. Situated on the Connecticut River, fifty miles from Long Island Sound. Connected with East Hartford, across the river, by a covered bridge, 1000 feet long. Population, 42,553. *Railroads—* Connecticut Central; Connecticut Valley— occupy same depot; Connecticut Western; New York & New England; New York, New Haven & Hartford— occupy same depot. *Business interests* - Manufacturing, mercantile and insurance. The city is for the most part compactly built, principally of brick and freestone.

Hotels— **Allyn House** ($3.50 per day), **United States, City** ($2.50 to 3.00 per day).

HASTINGS, Minn. Situated on the Mississippi River. Population, 3817.

Hotels **Foster, Tremont, St. Joe.**

HAVERHILL. Mass. Situated on the Merrimac River, at head of Navigation. Population, 18,475. *Railroad*--Boston & Maine. *Business interests*—Manufacturing, principally boots, shoes and hats.

Hotels—**Ætna, Central, City, Clinton, Eagle.**

HAZLETON, Pa. Population, 7546.
Hotels— **Central, Hazleton.**

HELENA, Ark. Situated on the Mississippi River, eighty miles below Memphis, Tenn. Population, 3600.
Hotel— **Shelby House.**

HELENA, Mon. Ter. Capital. Situated in Lewis and Clark County. Population, 3624.

This work is circulated gratuitously among prominent h ·tels of the United States.

CURTIS HOUSE

F. W. VOCKE, Proprietor,

MERIDEN. ✣ CONN.

$1.50 to $2.00 a Day. Liberal Discount.

FRANKLIN HOUSE

Cottage Place, near R. R. Depot,

STAMFORD, CONN.

FRED. BERG, Proprietor.

$1.00 per Day.   -   -   - $ .00 per Week.

MERIDEN HOUSE

While stopping at this House, have your WASHING DONE at the

MERIDEN ✦ STEAM ✦ LAUNDRY,

102 Crown Street, Meriden, Conn.

CALLED FOR AND DELIVERED FREE OF CHARGE.

ATLANTIC ⁂ GARDEN

Cor. Cheshire & Southington Roads from W. Main St.

JOHN DUIS, Proprietor.

SPLENDID HALL FOR PRIVATE PARTIES.
SHOOTING GALLERY CONNECTED.

Supper Furnished at Short Notice for Private Parties. Your patronage solicited.

Formerly at 7 and 9 State Street,   -   -   Meriden, Conn.

Thousand Island House,

ALEXANDRIA BAY, N. Y.

The THOUSAND ISLAND HOUSE is situated at Alexandria Bay, directly on the famous and historic river St. Lawrence—its scenery is absolutely unequaled. It has become a well-noted fact that there is actually no other region of resort in America combining so many attractive elements in Summer-time as the grand archipelago called the Thousand Islands, and drawing the line still closer, there is no other place having so many attractions, all points considered, as the Thousand Island House.

The grand and changeless St. Lawrence presents some features which are unique. Being the outflow of the great inland seas, its water is always perfectly pure. It is never subject to floods, and it has been noted by observant visitors that in midsummer among the Islands, and within a mile or so of the river, there is no dew at night (the fact is explained in the same manner as the existence of the well-known thermal belt along Niagara River). Malaria and hay fever unknown here.

The prevailing winds during the summer season sweep down, purified by their passage over the resinous Canadian forests, and over the wide expanse of the lake, reaching the nostrils of the fortunate guests—dry, bracing and cool; thus with its fresh and exhilarating atmosphere, the salubrity of the climate, the superb quality of its scenery, its attractions for angling and fishing, with boats of all kinds for those who desire, combined with the sumptuous accommodations of the THOUSAND ISLAND HOUSE, make it the most delightful inland resort in the northern regions of New York.

In fitting this house to suit the best custom of the country, especial regard for the comfort of families has been considered, and in its refitting, furnishing and all its details, it will be first-class.

A general reduction in prices for the coming season, especially during the months of June and September.

R. H. SOUTHGATE, Proprietor.

C. P. CLEMES, Manager.

Hotels—Cosmopolitan, International, Bon-Ton, Merchants.

HEMPSTEAD. Tex. Population, 1879.
Hotels— City, St. Charles, Sloan House, Texas House.

HENDERSON, Ky. Situated on the Ohio River. Population, 6573.
Hotels—Hord House, Commercial, Henderson, European.

HILLSDALE. Mich. Situated on the St. Joseph's River. Population, 3442.
Hotels—Smith's, Mosher's, Randell.

HOBOKEN, N. J. Situated on the Hudson River, opposite New York City. Population, 30,999. *Railroad*—Delaware, Lackawanna & Western. *Business interests*—Manufacturing and mercantile.
Hotels—Park, Bush's, Nagel, St. Clair.

HOLLIDAYSBURG, Pa. Situated on the Juniata River and Pennsylvania Canal. Population, 3139.
Hotels—American House, Logan House, Dannall's House.

HOLLY SPRINGS, Miss. Population, 2406.
Hotels—McComb House, Nuttall, Holly Springs.

HOLYOKE, Mass. Situated on the Connecticut River. Population, 21,851. *Railroads*—Connecticut River; New Haven & Northhampton—occupy separate depots. *Business interests*—Manufacturing.
Hotels—Windsor, Holyoke House, Samosett House.

HONESDALE, Pa. Population, 7000.

For advertising space in this work address the Na'ional Directory Co., New York City.

Hotels—**Allen House, Kipple House, Wayne County House.**

HOPKINSVILLE, Ky. Situated on the Little River. Population, 4250,
Hotels— **Phœnix, Cooper House.**

HORNELLSVILLE, N. Y. Situated on the Canisteo River. Population, 8200.
Hotels **Osborn, Nichols, Dellevan House.**

HOUSTON, Tex. Situated on Buffalo Bayou, an arm of Galveston Bay. Population, 18,646. *Railroads* Galveston, Harrisburg & San Antonio; Galveston, Houston & Henderson; International & Great Northern--occupy Union Depot; Galveston, Houston & Henderson; Houston & Texas Central—occupy same depot; Houston, East and West Texas; Texas Western; Texas & New Orleans occupy separate depots. *Business interests*—Commercial, manufacturing and mercantile. It is the railroad centre of Texas.
Hotels- **Capitol** ($3.00 to $3 50 per day), **Hutchins'.**

HOT SPRINGS, Ark.
Hotel- **Arlington.**

HUDSON. N. Y. Situated on the Hudson River, opposite Athens, N. Y. Population, 8770.
Hotels—**Central, City, Farmer's, St. Nicholas, Waldron, Worth, Hanor.**

HUDSON, Mich. Population, 3000.
Hotels—**Higgins, Comstock.**

HUNTINGDON, Pa. Situated on the Juniata River. Population, 4177.
Hotels—**Miller, Leister House, Franklin House.**

This work is circulated gratuitously among prominent hotels of the United States.

Thoroughly Renovated and Newly Furnished.

Mansion House

CLAPP & DUDLEY, Proprietors.

No. 510 Main Street, Springfield, Mass.

LADIES' ENTRANCE, 522 MAIN STREET.

ST. JAMES HOTEL

Cor. Broadway and 26th Street.

WM. M. CONNER, Prop'r

NEW YORK.

GRAND HOTEL
BROADWAY,

Corner of 31st Street,   NEW YORK.

HENRY MILFORD SMITH & SON,

PROPRIETORS.

HUNTSVILLE, Ala. Population, 6500.
Hotels—Huntsville, McGee's.

INDIANAPOLIS, Ind. Situated on the White River. Population, 75,074. *Railroads*—Cincinnati, Hamilton & Indianapolis; Cleveland, Columbus, Cincinnati & Indianapolis; Indiana, Bloomington & Western; Cincinnati, Indianapolis; St. Louis & Chicago; Wabash, St. Louis & Pacific; Indianapolis & St. Louis; Indianapolis & Vincennes;· Jeffersonville, Madison & Indianapolis; Chicago, St. Louis & Pittsburg; St. Louis, Vandalia, Terre Haute & Indianapolis—all roads centre in Union Depot, 400 feet long by 80 feet wide. *Business interests*— Mercantile and manufacturing, grain elevators, &c.

Hotels—**Bates, Grand, Denison** ($2.50 to $4 per day), **Mason, Occidental, Sherman, Spencer.**

IONIA, Mich. Situated on the Grand River. Population, 4700.
Hotels—**Bailey, Washington, Clarendon, Union, National, Dexter.**

IOWA CITY, Iowa. Situated on the Iowa River. Population, 8865.
Hotels—**St. James, Palace.**

IRONTON, O. Situated on the Ohio River. Population, 9000.
Hotels—**Sheridan** ($2 per day), **Irondale.**

ISHPEMING, Mich. Population, 6200.
Hotels—**Nelson House, Commercial House.**

ITHACA, N. Y. Situated on both sides of Cayuga Inlet, one mile from the head of Cayuga Lake. Population, 9140.

For advertising space in this work address the National Directory Co., New York City.

Hotels—**Ithaca, Clinton House, Tompkins House.**

JACKSON, Mich. Situated on both sides of the Grand River, at an elevation of 440 feet above Lake Michigan. Population, 16,105. *Railroads*—Fort Wayne & Jackson; Michigan Central (Grand River Valley and Air Line Divisions); Lake Shore & Michigan Southern; Jackson, Lansing & Saginaw—occupy separate depots. *Business interests*—Manufacturing and mercantile.

Hotels—**Hibbard, Hurd, Union, Commercial.**

JACKSON, Miss. Situated on the Pearl River. Population, 5472.

Hotels—**Edwards House, European, Spengler, Lawrence.**

JACKSON, Tenn. Situated on the Forked Deer River. Population, 5571.

Hotels—**Cavness, Lancaster, Merchants, Payne's, Robinson.**

JACKSONVILLE, Fla. Situated on the St. John's River. Population, 10,500. *Railroads*—Savannah, Florida & Western; Fernandina & Jacksonville; Florida Central & Western—occupy separate depots. *Business interests*—Mercantile, lumber, and centre of fruit growing district.

Hotels—**St James, Everett, St. Mark's, Windsor, Carleton, Duval.**

JACKSONVILLE, Ill. Population, 10,927. *Railroads*—Chicago & Alton; Peoria, Pekin & Jacksonville—occupy same depot; Jacksonville & Southeastern; Wabash, St. Louis & Pacific—occupy same depot. *Business interests*—Manufacturing, agricultural and mercantile.

Hotels—**Dunlap's, Park, Southern, Metropolitan.**

This work is circulated gratuitously among prominent hotels of the United States.

GEORGE M. DELANEY.   JAMES A. MCKANNA.

EVARTS ❋ HOUSE

OPPOSITE CITY PARK.

DELANEY & McKANNA, Props.

FREE 'BUS.

BURLINGTON, VT.

This House is newly Refurnished and fitted up, and no pains will be spared to make it First-Class in every department.

TERMS, $2 PER DAY.

JOS. McCLEAN,

Club House ⁑ and ⁑ Restaurant,

Nos. 35 & 37 WEST MAIN STREET,

Meriden, Conn.

JAMESTOWN, N. Y. Situated at the outlet of Chautauqua Lake. Population, 8514.
Hotels—Sherman ($2 to $3.50 per day).

JANESVILLE, Wis. Situated on the Rock River. Population, 9035.
Hotels—Myers' House, Grand Hotel, Davis House, Edwards House.

JEFFERSON CITY, Mo. Situated on the Missouri River. Population, 5420.
Hotels—Monroe, Central, Tennessee, Delmonico Restaurant, Railway Dining Hall (Union Depot).

JEFFERSON, Texas. Situated at the head of navigation on Big Cyprus Bayou. Population, 8000.
Hotels—Excelsior, Pruitt's.

JEFFERSON, Wis. Situated near Rock River. Population, 2115.
Hotels—Sawyer, Jefferson.

JEFFERSONVILLE, Ind. Situated on the Ohio River, opposite Louisville, Ky. Population, 10,422. *Railroads*—Jeffersonville, Madison & Indianapolis; Ohio & Mississippi—occupy same depot; Jeffersonville, Louisville & New Albany—separate depot. *Business interests*—Mercantile, manufacturing, ship-yards, &c.
Hotels—National, Falls City House, Falls View House, Sherman.

JERSEY CITY, N. J. Situated on the Hudson River, at its entrance into New York Bay, opposite New York City. Population, 120,728. *Railroads*—New York, Lake Erie & Western; New York & Greenwood Lake; New Jersey & New York—occupy same depot; Lehigh

For advertising space in this work address the National Directory Co., New York City.

Valley; New Jersey Midland; Pennsylvania; New York, West Shore & Buffalo—occupy same depot; Central of New Jersey—occupies separate depot. *Business interests*—Manufacturing and commercial.
Hotel—**Taylor's.**

JOHNSTOWN, Pa. Situated on the Conemaugh River. Population, 22,000. *Railroads*—Pennsylvania; Somerset & Cambria Branch of Baltimore & Ohio occupy separate depots. *Business interests*—Manufacturing.
Hotels—**Mansion, Merchants, Hulbert House, Cambria Club House.**

JOHNSTOWN, N. Y. Population, 5200.
Hotels—**Sir William Johnson, Harden, Railroad, Langfield, Dixon.**

JOLIET, Ill. Situated on the Desplaines River and Illinois and Michigan Canal. Population, 16,145. *Railroads*—Chicago & Alton; Chicago, Pekin and Southwestern—occupy same depot; Chicago, Rock Island & Pacific; Michigan Central—occupy separate depots. *Business interests*—Stone quarries, manufacturing, mercantile, &c.
Hotels—**St. Nicholas, Auburn, National, Robertson House.**

JOPLIN, Mo. Population, 7038.
Hotels—**Joplin, Pacific, St. James, Commercial, Jasper, Allington.**

JUNCTION CITY, Kan. Situated near the confluence of the Republican and Smoky Hill Rivers. Population, 2670.
Hotels—**Bartell, Pacific, Pershall.**

KALAMAZOO, Mich. Situated on the Kalamazoo

This work is circulated gratuitously among prominent h tels of the United States.

Middletown, Conn.

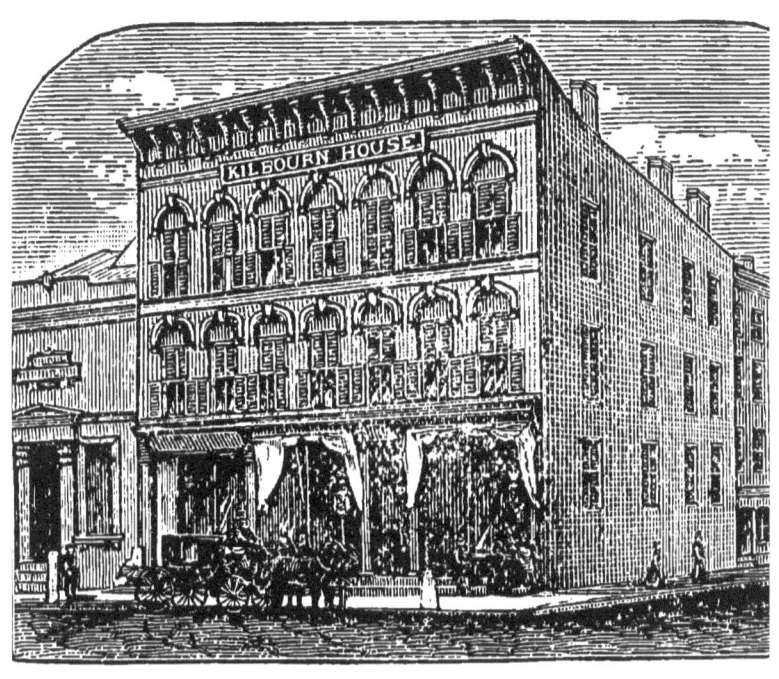

Terms per Day, $1.50 and $2.00.

CENTRAL LOCATION

Hotel St. Stephen.

EUROPEAN PLAN.

42 to 52 East Eleventh Street, N. Y.

BET. BROADWAY AND UNIVERSITY PLACE.

W. D. RYDER, Proprietor.

Single Rooms, $1.00 per Day and Upward.

Double Rooms, $2.00 per Day and Upward.

River. Population, 11,937. *Railroads*—Grand Rapids & Indiana; Lake Shore & Michigan Southern; Michigan Central—all roads occupy separate depots. Grand Rapids & Indiana and Michigan Central connect at Junction. *Business interests*—Mercantile, manufacturing and agricultural.

Hotels—**The Burdick House, American, Kalamazoo House.**

KANKAKEE, Ill. Situated on the Kankakee River. Population, 6000.

Hotels—**Commercial, City, Kankakee.**

KANSAS CITY, Mo. Situated on the Missouri River. Population, 55,813. *Railroads*—Atchison, Topeka & Santa Fé; Chicago & Alton; Hannibal & St. Joseph; Kansas City & Eastern; Kansas City, Fort Scott & Gulf; Kansas Pacific; Kansas City; Lawrence & Southern; Kansas City, St. Joseph & Council Bluffs; Missouri Pacific; Wabash, St. Louis & Pacific; Chicago, Rock Island & Pacific—all roads occupy Union Depot. *Bank*—Bank of Kansas City. *Business interests*—Mercantile, packing beef and pork, grain, &c.

Hotels—**Coates House, St. James, Metropolitan, Pacific, Centropolis.**

KEENE, N. H. Situated on the Ashuelot River. Population, 6780.

Hotels—**Cheshire, Eagle, City.**

KENOSHA, Wis. Situated on Lake Michigan, at the mouth of Kenosha River. Population, 5043.

Hotel—**Grant House ($2 per day).**

KENTON, O. Situated on the Scioto River. Population, 4600.

For advertising space in this work address the National Directory Co., New York City.

Hotels—Dugan House, Franklin House.

KEOKUK, Iowa. Situated on the Mississippi River. Population, 12,117. *Railroads*—Chicago, Burlington & Quincy; Chicago, Rock Island & Pacific; St. Louis, Keokuk & Northwestern; Wabash, St. Louis & Pacific—all roads occupy same depot. *Business interests*—Commercial, mercantile, agricultural and manufacturing.

Hotels—Patterson, Commercial, La Clede, Barrett, Clyde, St. Louis.

KINGSTON, N. Y. Population, 18,342. The city of Kingston includes Kingston proper and Rondout, the latter situated on Rondout Creek, opposite Rhinebeck, one mile above the Hudson River. *Railroads*—Ulster & Delaware; Walkill Valley; West Shore & Buffalo—occupy separate depots in Kingston proper, but the same depot in Rondout. *Business interests*—Manufacturing and mercantile.

Hotels—in Rondout, Mansion, Excelsior; in Kingston, Brown's, Eagle.

KINGSTON, Ont. On the St. Lawrence River, at the foot of Lake Ontario. Population, 14,500. *Railroads*—Grand Trunk; Kingston & Pembroke—occupy separate depots. *Business interests*—Commercial, manufacturing and mercantile.

Hotels—Windsor, British-American, Anglo-American, City.

KNOXVILLE, Tenn. Situated on the Tennessee River. Population, 13,928. *Railroads*—East Tennessee, Virginia & Georgia; Knoxville & Charleston; Knoxville & Ohio—all roads occupy same depot. *Business interests*—Manufacturing and mercantile.

This work is circulated gratuitously among prominent hotels of the United States.

EVERETT'S HOTEL
AND
Grand Dining Rooms.

-- EUROPEAN PLAN --

Nos. 102, 104 & 106 Vesey Street,

(Through to 98 Barclay Street),

Bet. Washington and West Sts.   **NEW YORK.**

Opposite recent newly-built Washington Market.

ENTIRE HOUSE OPEN DAY AND NIGHT, and lighted in its entirety by the Edison system at a cost of Ten Thousand Dollars for the plant of Isolated Lighting.

Two Hundred Elegantly Furnished Rooms—50c., 75c. and $1 per day; $2, $3 and $5 per week, and upward, according to location, &c.

The grandeur displayed within the marble walls of this Establishment is unsurpassed.

THE CUISINE has no auperior, both in Edibles and Service. Charges reasonable, and in keeping with the best elements of a first-class American Hotel and Dining Room.

SAMUEL H. EVERETT, Prop.

Grand Union Hotel

Opposite Grand Central Depot, N. Y. City.

IMPORTANT.

Passengers arriving in the City of New York via Grand Central Depot, save $3 Carriage Hire and Transfer of Baggage by stopping at the GRAND UNION HOTEL, opposite said depot.

Passengers arriving by West Shore Railroad, via Weehawken Ferry, by taking the 42d Street Horse Cars at Ferry entrance, reach Grand Union Hotel in ten minutes for 5 cents, and save $3 Carriage Hire.

Six hundred Elegant Rooms, $1 and upwards per day. European Plan. Elevators, Restaurant, Cafe, Lunch and Wine Rooms supplied with the best.

Prices moderate. Families can live better and for less money at the Grand Union than at any other strictly first-class hotel in the city. Guests' baggage delivered to and from Grand Central Depot, free.

Hotels—Schubert's, Hattie, Atkin, Lamar.

KOKOMO, Ind. Population, 4000.
Hotels—Clinton House, Central.

LA CROSSE. Wis. Situated on the Mississippi River. Population, 14,505. *Railroads*—Chicago, Milwaukee & St. Paul; Chicago & Northwestern; Green Bay, Winona & St. Paul. *Business interests*—Mercantile, manufacturing, logs, lumber and flour milling.
Hotels—International, Cameron House.

LAFAYETTE, Ind. Situated on the Wabash River and the Wabash and Erie Canal. Population, 14,600. *Railroads*—Cincinnati, Lafayette & Chicago; Cincinnati, Indianapolis, St. Louis & Chicago; Lake Erie & Western—occupy same depot; Louisville, New Albany & Chicago; Wabash, St. Louis & Pacific—occupy separate depots. *Business interests*—Mercantile, manufacturing and agricultural.
Hotels—Bramble, Germania, Lahr, Star City, St. Nicholas.

LAMBERTVILLE, N. J. Situated on the Delaware River, opposite New Hope, Pa. Population, 4300.
Hotels—Lambertville, Belmont, Union.

LANCASTER, O. Situated on the Hocking River. Population, 7000.
Hotels—Mithoff, Tallmadge, American.

LANCASTER, Pa. Population, 25,769. *Railroads*—Pennsylvania; Philadelphia & Reading—occupy separate depots. *Business interests*—Manufacturing, agricultural and mercantile.
Hotels—Grape, Hiester, Steven's, Casper House.

For advertising space in this work address the National Directory Co., New York City.

LANSING, Mich. Capital of State. Situated at the confluence of the Grand and Cedar Rivers. Population, 8326.
Hotels—Hudson House, Lansing House, Chapman, Everett, Eichols, and Franklin House at North Lansing,

LAPEER, Mich. Situated on the Flint River. Population, 3479.
Hotels—Abrams House, Marshall House, American, Farmer's Home.

LA PORTE, Ind. Situated on Clear Lake. Population, 6189.
Hotels—Teegarden House, Myers House.

LARAMIE, Wy. Situated on the Laramie River. Population, 3246.
Hotels—Frontier, Thornburgh, New York, Mechanics, Worths.

LAREDO, Tex. Situated on eastern bank of the Rio Grande River. Population, 3521.
Hotels—Laredo, St. Charles, Wilson, Rockport.

LA SALLE, Ill. Situated on the Illinois River, at the head of navigation, and the terminus of the Illinois & Michigan Canal. Population, 7250.
Hotels—Harrison, La Salle.

LAWRENCE, Kan. Situated on the Kansas River. Population, 8523.
Hotels—Eldridge, Durfee, Lawrence, Commercial, Laclede, Pennsylvania.

LAWRENCE, Mass. Situated on the Merrimac River. Population, 39,178. *Railroads*—Boston & Maine, Boston

---

This work is circulated gratuitously among prominent hotels of the United States.

& Lowell—occupy separate depots; Eastern; Manchester & Lawrence—occupy same depot. *Business interests—* Manufacturing.

Hotels—**Franklin, Brunswick, Central, Essex.**

LEAVENWORTH, Kan. Situated on the Missouri River. Population, 16,550. *Railroads*—Chicago, Rock Island & Pacific; Kansas Central; Union Pacific (K. P. Div.); Missouri Pacific—occupy same depot; Kansas City, St. Joseph & Council Bluffs—occupies separate depot. *Bank*—First National. *Business interests*—Manufacturing, commercial, grain and cattle shipping.

Hotels—**Planter's** (Rates, $2.00 and $2.50 per day), **Delmonico, Continental.**

LEBANON, Pa. Population, 8787.

Hotels—**Eagle, Central, Lebanon Valley.**

LEE, Mass. Situated on Housatonic River. Population, 3038.

Hotels—**Morgan House, Norton House.**

LE MARS, Ia. Situated at junction of Illinois Central & Chicago, St. Paul, Minneapolis & Omaha Railroads. Population, 2073.

Hotel—**Revere.**

LEWISBURG, Pa. Situated on the west branch of the Susquehanna River. Population, 3498.

Hotels—**Cameron House, American House.**

LEWISTON, Me. Situated on the Androscoggin River. Population, 19,083. *Railroads*—Maine Central—. Upper and Lower Stations; Grand Trunk—three separate depots. *Business interests*—Manufacturing.

Hotels—**DeWitt House, Marston House.**

For advertising space in this work address the National Directory Co., New York City.

LEWISTOWN, Pa. Situated on the Juniata River and Canal. Population, 3347.
Hotels—National, Union, Coleman.

LEXINGTON, Ky. Situated on the Town Fork of the Elk Horn River. Population, 16,656. *Railroads*—Cincinnati Southern; Kentucky Central; Louisville, Cincinnati & Lexington; Chesapeake and Ohio—occupy separate depots. *Business interests*—Manufacturing (chiefly whiskey), stock raising, mercantile, etc.
Hotels—Phœnix, St. Nicholas, Ashland.

LEXINGTON, Mo. Population, 4060.
Hotels—City, Commercial, Long's.

LIMA, O. Situated on the Ottawa River. Population, 8000.
Hotels—French, Lima, Burnett, Globe.

LINCOLN, Ill. Population. 5528.
Hotels—Commercial, Spitley, Lincoln.

LINCOLN, Neb. Capital of State. Population, 13,004. *Railroads*—Burlington and Missouri River in Nebraska; Union Pacific—occupy separate depots. *Business interests*—Manufacturing, mercantile and agricultural.
Hotel—Commercial.

LITCHFIELD, Ill. Population, 4307.
Hotels—Phœnix, Central, Palace, Cottage, Bowlby House.

LITTLE FALLS, N. Y. Situated on both sides of the Mohawk River. Population, 6940.
Hotels—Grand Central, Hinchman, Girvan, Bradford.

LITTLE ROCK, Ark. Capital of State. Situated on the Arkansas River. Population, 13,185. *Railroads*—

This work is circulated gratuitously among prominent hotels of the United States.

European Plan. **TAYLOR'S HOTEL** Jersey City, N. J.

Directly opposite Pennsylvania R. R. Passenger Depot, and overlooking the Hudson River. 200 Rooms, $1.00 and upwards per day.

GEO. B. De REVERE, Proprietor.

NOTICE.

The Second Annual Issue of *Thompson's Wholesale Druggists' and Drug Specialists' Directory*, has just been published. It gives an Accurate List of Importers, Manufacturers, Jobbers, Wholesale Dealers, and Specialists in the Drug and kindred trades. As a Reference Book it is especially adapted to the Retail Trade. Price, $1.00. Published by the

NATIONAL DIRECTORY CO.,
New York City.

Little Rock & Fort Smith; Little Rock & Arkansas City —occupy separate depots; Memphis & Little Rock; St. Louis, Iron Mountain & Southern—occupy same depot. *Business interests*—Mercantile, manufacturing, cotton and cotton seed. Cross & Diver's stages, carrying U. S. mails for Pine Bluff and Monticello, connect with all trains.

Hotels—**Capitol**, on European plan, with first-class restaurant, located in business centre; **Grand Central, Gleason's** (at depot), **Atlantic, Adams.**

LIVINGSTON, Montana. Situated at the foot of the Belt Mountains where the Northern Pacific Railroad last crosses the Yellowstone River, and is about half way from the Great Lakes to the Pacific Coast; at this point a branch road leaves the main line and runs in a southerly direction to the Yellowstone National Park. Large round houses and railroad shops are located at this point.

Hotels –**Livingston, Merchant's, Brunswick, Metropolitan.**

LOCK HAVEN, Pa. Situated on the Susquehanna River, and West Branch Canal. Population, 9000.

Hotels—**Fallon House, Montour, Irvin.**

LOCKPORT, N. Y. Located on the Erie Canal. Population, 13,522. *Railroads*—New York Central & Hudson River; Lockport & Buffalo; New York, Lake Erie & Western—occupy separate depots. *Business interests*—Manufacturing, mercantile, fruit growing, boat building,

Hotels—**American, Judson, McLean's.**

LOGANSPORT, Ind. Situated on the Wabash and Eel Rivers. Population, 11,198. *Railroads*—Eel River;

For advertising space in this work address the Na'ional Directory Co., New York City.

Logansport, Terre Haute & Indianapolis—occupy same depot; Pittsburgh, Cincinnati & St. Louis; Wabash, St. Louis & Pacific—occupy separate depots. *Business interests*—Manufacturing, mercantile and agricultural.
Hotels—**Windsor, Murdock, Gehring, Barnett City.**

LONDON, Ont. Situated on the Thames River. Population, 26,000. *Railroads*—Grand Trunk; Great Western & Canada—occupy separate depots. *Business interest*—Manufacturing.
Hotels—**Tecumseh, Grigg, River, City, Western, Strong's, Cousin's, Brittania.**

LOS ANGELES, Cal. Situated on the Los Angeles River. Population, 11,311. *Railroad*—Southern Pacific. *Business interests*—Fruit growing and wine manufacture. It is beautifully situated.
Hotels—**Cosmopolitan, Pico House, Grand Central, United States, White House.**

LOUISIANA, Mo. Situated on the Mississippi River. Population, 4325.
Hotels—**La Clede, City, West House.**

LOUISVILLE, Ky. Situated on the Ohio River. A port of entry. Population, 123,625. *Railroads*—Jeffersonville, Madison & Indianapolis, Louisville, New Albany & Chicago; Ohio & Mississippi—occupy same depot; Louisville & Nashville, and its branches occupy separate depots; Louisville, Evansville & St. Louis R'y; Chesapeake & Ohio, and Chesapeake, Ohio & Southwestern R.R.'s. Railroad and Ferry to Jeffersonville, Ind., and New Albany, Ind. Regular Steamboat Lines to all points on the Ohio and confluent streams. *Business interests*—

This work is circulated gratuitously among prominent hotels of the United States.

TEMPLE & PUTNEY, ◁ROSSMORE HOTEL▷ 41st & 42d Sts., N. Y.
Proprietors,

Five minutes from Grand Central and West Shore Depots by 42d St. Cross-town Cars.

AMERICAN AND EUROPEAN PLAN.

Rooms, with Board, - - - $3.00 and $3.50 per Day.
Rooms, without Board, - - - $1.00 per Day and upwards.

☞ Coolest and Best Ventilated Hotel in the City. ☜ Elegant new Gentlemen's Cafe in connection with Hotel.

Madison Sq. FIFTH AVENUE HOTEL New York.

☞ The largest, best appointed and most liberally managed Hotel in New York, with the most central and delightful location.

HITCHCOCK, DARLING & CO., Proprietors.

Mercantile and manufacturing—leading interests of the latter are, tobacco, whiskey, plows and leather.

Hotels—Galt House, Louisville, Standiford, Rufer's, Willard, Alexander's, Fifth Avenue, Balmer's, St. Cloud, New Southern.

LOWELL, Mass. Situated at the confluence of the Merrimack and Concord Rivers. Population, 59,485. *Railroads*—Boston & Lowell; Old Colony; Nashua & Lowell—occupy same depot; Boston & Maine—occupies separate depot. *Business interests*—Manufacturing.

Hotels—Washington, Merrimack, American, Dresser House.

LYNCHBURGH, Va. Situated on the James River. Population, 20,500. *Railroads*—Norfolk & Western; Va. Midland; Lynchburgh & Danville; Richmond & Alleghany—occupy same depot. *Business interests*—Tobacco manufacturing and mercantile.

Hotels—Arlington, Norvell, Lynch House.

LYNN, Mass. Situated on Massachusetts Bay. Population, 38,284. *Railroads*—Boston, Revere Beach & Lynn; Eastern—occupy separate depots. *Business interests*—Manufacturing boots and shoes. Noted as a pleasure resort.

Hotels—Kirtland, Sagamon, Brunswick, Auburn, Crawford.

LYONS, Ia. Situated on the Mississippi River. Population, 4000.

Hotels—American, Union, Transit, City.

LYONS, N. Y. Located on the Erie Canal. Population, 4200.

For advertising space in this work address the National Directory Co., New York City.

Hotels—Congress Hall, Graham, Exchange, National, Central, Lyons.

McKEESPORT, Pa. Situated at the confluence of the Allegheny & Youghiogheny Rivers, fifteen miles southeast of Pittsburg. Population, 7997.
Hotels—National, Montezuma, White House, Centennial.

MACON, Ga. Situated on both sides of the Ocmulgee River, at the head of navigation. Population, 12,748. *Railroads*—Central of Georgia (Main Line and Southwestern Div.); Georgia; Macon & Brunswick—occupy same depot. *Business interests*—Mercantile and Manufacturing. The cotton mart and distributing point for southern and southwestern Georgia and Eastern Alabama.
Hotels—Brown's, Lanier, National, Stubblefield.

MACON CITY, Mo. Population, 3100.
Hotels—Wabash, City, Merchants'.

MADISON, Ind. Situated on the Ohio River. Population, 9009.
Hotels—Central, Continental, Centennial, Western, Broadway, William Tell House.

MADISON, Wis. Situated on an isthmus separating Lakes Mendota and Monona. Population, 10,325. *Railroads*—Chicago & North-Western; Chicago, Milwaukee & St. Paul--occupy separate depots. *Business interests*—Mercantile and manufacturing.
Hotels--Park, Capital, Vilas, Capitol.

MAHANOY CITY, Pa. Population, 7350.
Hotels—Eagle, Merchants', Mansion House.

This work is circulated gratuitously among prominent hotels of the United States.

Westminster Hotel

NEW YORK CITY.

Irving Place and 16th St., near Union Square.

W. C. SCHENCK, Prop.

The Westminster is conducted on the American plan, and is practically fire-proof. The Hotel is furnished and fitted in the most modern and luxurious style, and its cuisine will be maintained at the highest standard of excellence.

The location is central, and convenient to all the large retail stores and places of amusement.

Strangers visiting the city, either on business or pleasure, will find comfort and polite attention at the Westminster.

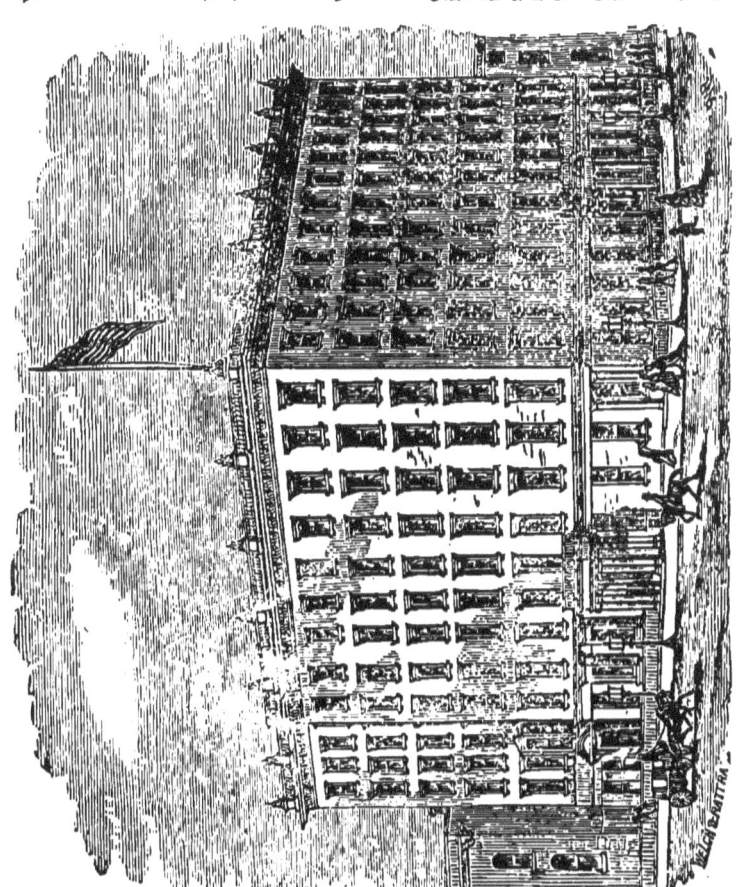

St. Nicholas Hotel

WASHINGTON PLACE,

BROADWAY and MERCER STREET,

New York

AMERICAN PLAN

$2.50 per Day.

JULIUS A. ROBINSON, Proprietor.

MALDEN, Mass. Situated on the Malden River. Population, 12,017. *Railroads*—Boston & Maine; Eastern—occupy separate depots. *Business interest*—Manufacturing; Boston Rubber Shoe Co., employs 1500 men, women and boys.

Hotels—**Evelyn, Howard, Pratt's.**

MANCHESTER, N. H. Situated on the Merrimac River. Population, 32,630. *Railroads*—Concord; Concord & Portsmouth; Manchester & Lawrence; Manchester & North Weare—occupy same depot. *Business interests*—Manufacturing.

The corporate city limits include the villages of Pascataquog and Amoskeag (commonly called "Squag" and "Skeag").

Hotels—**Manchester, City, Chandler, Granite.**

MANCHESTER, Va. Situated on the James River, opposite Richmond. Population, 6036.

Hotels—(two).

MANDAN, Dak. Situated on the western bank of the Missouri River. The Northern Pacific R. R. crosses the river at this point on a three-span iron bridge costing $150,000. The change between mountain and central time is made at this point.

Hotels—**Inter-Ocean, Commercial, Mandan House, St. Elmo.**

MANITOWOC, Wis. Situated on Lake Michigan, at the mouth of Manitowoc River. Population, 6563.

Hotels—**North-western, Windiate, Williams' St. Charles.**

MANKATO, Minn. Population, 6000. After the terrible Indian massacre of 1862, the pioneer troops under

For advertising space in this work address the National Directory Co., New York City.

General Sibley brought 2,500 prisoners to Mankato for military trial. Of these, 303 were sentenced to death. But President Lnicoln interceded, and after a personal examination of all the testimony, ordered the sentence to be carried out only in such instances as murder, aggravated by outrages on white women and children. In pursuance of this order, 37 of the condemed were hanged. The execution took place December 19th, 1862, on a long prairie ridge south-west of the town. All the gallows were operated simultaneously by the pulling of a single rope; a soldier, whose entire family had been murdered by the savages, was executioner. Mankato has at present two hotels, three weekly newspapers, a state normal school and a large Catholic college. There are several oil mills, foundries and machine shops and a large argricultural trade is carried on.

MANSFIELD, O. Situated on the Rocky Fork of the Mohican River. Population. 9992.

Hotels—**Wiler** ($2.00 per day), **St. James** ($2.00 per day), **American, Clifton, European, Tremont House.**

MARBLEHEAD, Mass. Situated on Marblehead Bay. Population, 7400.

Hotels—**Clifton House, Union House, Bell's House, Bailey's House, Devereux Mansion, Smiths' Mansion.**

MARIETTA, O. Situated on the Ohio River, at the mouth of the Muskingum River. Population, 6000.

Hotels—**St. Cloud, National House, Bizante, United States.**

MARION, Ala. Population, 2750.
Hotel—**The King House.**

This work is circulated gratuitously among prominent hotels of the United States.

MARLBORO, Mass. Population, 10,126. *Railroads* —Old Colony, Fitchburg,—occupy separate depots. *Business interests*—Boot and shoe manufacturing, machinery and dye manufacture.
Hotels—Central, Marlboro, Gates, Temple.

MARSHALL, Mich. Situated on the Kalamazoo River. Population, 3806.
Hotels—Tremont, Tontine, Forbes House.

MARSHALL, Tex. Population, 5657.
Hotel—Capitol.

MARSHALLTOWN, Ia. Situated one mile from the Iowa River. Population, 6400.
Hotel—Tremont.

MARTINSBURG, W. Va. Population, 6384.
Hotels—Grand Central, Continental.

MARQUETTE, Mich. Situated on the south shore of Lake Superior. Population, 6510.
Hotels—Summit, Tremont.

MARYSVILLE, Cal. Population, 4443.
Hotels—Western, United States.

MASSILLON, O. Situated on the Tuscarawas River and Ohio Canal. Population, 6754.
Hotels—Park, Farmers.

MATTOON, Ill. Population, 6000.
Hotels—Dole, Essex, City, Everett.

MAUCH CHUNK, Pa. Situated on the Lehigh River, at the mouth of Mauch Chunk Creek. Population; 5603.
Hotels—American, Mansion House.

For advertising space in this work address the National Directory Co., New York City.

MAYSVILLE, Ky. Situated on the Ohio River, sixty-one miles above Cincinnati, and seventy miles north-east of Lexington. Population, 6500.
Hotels—Central, European, Germania, Schatzman.

MAYWOOD, Ill. One of the most prosperous suburbs of the city of Chicago, situated on the west bank of the Desplaines River, ten miles from the heart of the city. Population, 1500. The Chicago Scraper and Ditcher Co., employing about two hundred men, is situated here, also extensive paimt works. There is one first-class hotel, with livery stable attached; several churches and good educational advantages.

MEADVILLE, Pa. Population, 10,500. *Railroad*— New York, Pennsylvania & Ohio. *Business interests*—Mercantile, manufacturing and petroleum.
Hotels—McHenry, Commercial ($2.00 per day), Central, Budd House.

MEDFORD, Mass. Population. 7654.
Hotels—Medford, Mystic, Simpson.

MEMPHIS, Tenn. Situated on the Mississippi River. A port of entry. Population, 33,593. *Railroads*—Louisville & Nashville, Memphis & Little Rock,—occupy same depot; Memphis & Charleston, Mississippi & Tennessee, Chesapeake & Ohio, (South-western Div.)—occupy separate depots. Through passengers transferred to and from Memphis & Charleston and Memphis & Little Rock depots without change of cars. *Business interests*— Commercial, mercantile and argricultural; great cotton port.
Hotels—New Clarendon, Peabody, Gaston, Worsham, Cochran.

This work is circulated gratuitously among prominent hotels of the United States.

MENDOTA, Ill. Population, 3750.
Hotels—Depot House, St. James, Mendota, Warner House, National.

MERIDIAN, Miss. Population, 4013.
Hotels—Winthrop, Ragsdale, European, Central, Delmonico's.

MERIDEN, Ct. Population, 18,340. *Railroad*—New York, New Haven & Hartford. *Business interests*—Manufacturing.
Hotels—Meriden, Byxbee, Curtis House.

MICHIGAN CITY, Ind. Situated on Lake Michigan. Population, 7500.
Hotels—Jewell House, St. Nicholas, Union (European).

MIDDLETOWN, Ct. Situated on the Connecticut River. A port of entry. Population, 11,731. *Railroads* —Boston & New York Air-Line, Connecticut Valley,— separate depots; New York, New Haven & Hartford,— occupies separate depot. *Business interests*—Manufacturing, mercantile and argricultural.
Hotels—Clarendon, Kilbourn House, McDonough House.

MIDDLETOWN, N. Y. Population, 8700.
Hotels—Grand Central, Taylor House, Union House.

MILES CITY, Montana. Situated on the Northern Pacific Railroad at the junction of the Tongue River with Yellow Stone.
Hotels—Inter-Ocean, Commercial, Merchants.

MILFORD, Mass. Situated on the Charles River. Population, 9310.

For advertising space in this work a ldress the National Directory Co., New York City.

Hotels—**Mansion, Milford.**

MILLVILLE, N. J. Situated on the Maurice River, at the head of Navigation. Population, 8000.
Hotels—**Doughty House, Franklin House.**

MILTON, Pa. Situated on the west branch of the Susquehanna River and West Branch Canal. Population, 2500.
Hotels—**Broadway, Riverside.**

MILWAUKEE, Wis. Situated on Lake Michigan and the Milwaukee River; also, near the mouth of Menomonee River. A port of entry. Population, 115,578. *Railroads*—Chicago & Northwestern; Milwaukee, Lake Shore & Western—occupy same depot; Chicago, Milwaukee & St. Paul; Wisconsin Central—occupy same depot. *Business interests*—Commercial, manufacturing and mercantile.
Hotels—**Plankinton** ($2 to $4 per day), **Axtill House** ($2 per day).

MINERSVILLE, Pa. Situated on the west branch of the Schuylkill River. Population, 3500.
Hotels—**Keystone, Washington House, Exchange, United States, Union House.**

MINNEAPOLIS, Minn. Situated on both sides of the Mississippi River, at the Falls of St. Anthony, the two divisions, east and west, connected by four magnificent bridges. Located at the foot of navigation of the Upper Mississippi, it is a large manufacturing point, possessing one of the finest and largest available water-powers in the world. Population, 46,877. *Railroads*—Minneapolis & St. Louis; St. Paul, Minneapolis & Mani-

---

This work is circulated gratuitously among prominent hotels of the United States.

FINE WHISKIES

Our Establishment, GIBSONTON MILLS, on the Monongahela River, with its extensive MALT HOUSE, gives us unequaled facilities for making

PURE RYE and BARLEY MALT WHISKIES,

Of superior Quality, from Kiln-dried Rye and Barley Malt.

These Whiskies are highly improved by age, and their unrivaled quality is widely known and appreciated.

MOORE & SINNOTT,
SUCCESSORS TO

JOHN GIBSON'S SON & CO.

New England Agency, 162 State St.

FOR SALE BY DRUGGISTS AND RELIABLE DEALERS

JAMES McCREERY & CO.

Invite the attention of Out-of-Town Buyers to their Large and Attractive Stock of

RICH SILKS, VELVETS, PLUSHES,

WOOL DRESS GOODS, LACES,

HOSIERY, GLOVES, SUITS, WRAPS,

LADIES' and CHILDREN'S UNDERWEAR,

UPHOLSTERY, HOUSEKEEPING GOODS, &c.

We have in all our respective Departments a full line of Medium Priced goods to the Finest Imported.

☞ Orders per Mail or Express receive prompt attention.

SILK PATCH WORK.

Packages of twenty pieces, 4½ x 4½, choice patterns, one dollar per package.

JAMES McCREERY & CO.,
Broadway and 11th Street, New York.

toba; Chicago, St. Paul, Minneapolis & Omaha—occupy same depot; Chicago, Milwaukee & St. Paul—occupy separate depot. *Business interests* —Manufacturing, lumber and agricultural.

Hotels—**West House, Nicollet** (rates, $3 and $4 per day), **Clark,** (rates $2 per day), **St. James, National, Windsor, Bellevue.**

MOBILE, Ala. Situated on Mobile Bay, at the mouth of Mobile River. A port of entry. Population, 31,205. *Railroads*—Louisville & Nashville; Mobile & Ohio; New Orleans & Mobile; Mobile & Spring Hill—occupy same depot; Mobile & Alabama Grand Trunk, occupies separate depot. *Business interests*—Commercial, cotton, etc.,

Hotels—**Battle House** ($2 to $3 50 per day), **St. James'** ($2 to $2.50 per day).

MOLINE, Ill. Situated on the Mississippi River. Population, 7740.

Hotels—**Keator, Peals, Revere, American, Bridge.**

MONMOUTH, Ill. Population, 5004.
Hotels—**Baldwin, Commercial, Windsor.**

MONROE, Mich. Situated on both sides of the Raisin River, near its entrance into Lake Erie. Population, 5007.

Hotel—**Park.**

MONROE, Wis. Population, 4350.
Hotels—**United States, Warfield, City, Monroe.**

Montgomery, Ala. Situated on the Alabama River. Population, 16,714. *Railroads*—Louisville & Nashville; Mobile & Montgomery; Montgomery & Eufaula; West-

---

For advertising space in this work address the National Directory Co., New York City.

ern Alabama—occupy same depot. *Business interests—* Mercantile and agricultural.
Hotels—**The Windsor, Exchange.**

MONTPELIER, Vt. Situated on the Winooski River. Population, 3225.
Hotels—**American, Bishop's, Pavilion, Union.**

MONTREAL, Quebec. Situated on the south side of Island Montreal, in the St. Lawrence River. Population, 140, 747. *Railroads*—Grand Trunk; South-eastern; Quebec, Montreal, Ottawa & Occidental—all occupy separate depots. *Business interests*—Mercantile and manufacturing.
Hotels—**Windsor, Ottawa, Abion, St. Lawrence Hall.**

MOOREHEAD, Minn. Situated on the east bank of the Red River, and on western boundary of the State. *Railroads*—Northern Pacific; St. Paul, Minneapolis & Manitoba; Moorhead & Northern. *Business interests*— Largely manufacturing with good facilities for general merchandise.
Hotels—**Grand Pacific, Jay Cook, Central, Key City, St. Charles.**

MORRISTOWN, N. J. Situated on the Whippany River. Population, 5446.
Hotels—**Mansion House, United States, Farmer's, Avenue House, Park House.**

MOUNT CLEMENS, Mich. Situated on Clinton River, three and a half miles from Lake St. Clair. Population, 3057.
Hotel—**Avery.**

This work is circulated gratuitously among prominent hotels of the United States.

Foreign Offices and Factories:

PARIS, RUDOLSTADT, LIMOGES,
———CARLSBAD and STEINSCHONAU.

L. STRAUS & SONS,

IMPORTERS OF

Pottery  Glassware

FROM ALL COUNTRIES,

42, 44 and 46 Warren Street, N. Y.

WE HAVE A SPECIAL DEPARTMENT DEVOTED TO THE
WANTS IN OUR LINE OF HOTELS, CLUBS,
YACHTS AND STEAMSHIPS.

1835–1885.

Foster, Merriam & Co.

MERIDEN, CONN.

JOHN SUTLIFF, PREST.   GEO. C. MERRIAM, SECY. & TREAS.

AGENCIES:

Grand Rapids, Mich., - - 19 Pearl Street.
  JOSHUA SPEED, Manager.
San Francisco, Cal., - 109 California Street.
  JOHN D. FRENCH, Manager.
New York City, - - - 225 Canal Street.
  W. ZERFASS, Manager.

MANUFACTURERS OF

Cabinet Hardware, Casters, Drawer Pulls, Escutcheons, Toilet Screws, Hat and Coat Hooks, Hall Stand Pins, Mirror Brackets, Candle Brackets, Brass Tables, Chair and Stool Screws, Furniture Fenders, &c., &c.

MOUNT HOLLY, N. J. Population, 4621.
Hotels—Arcade, Smith's, Washington House.
MOUNT PLEASANT, Ia. Population, 4490.
Hotels—Brazelton, Harlem, Wiggin's.
MOUNT PLEASANT, Mich. Population, 2000.
Hotels—Bennett, Exchange, Peninsular, Hastings, Bamber.
MOUNT VERNON, O. Situated on the Kokosing River. Population, 5400.
Hotels—Curtis, Bergen, Rowley.
MUNCIE, Ind. Situated on the White River. Population, 5221.
Hotels—Haines House, Kirby House.
MURFREESBORO, Tenn. Population, 4030.
Hotels—Ready, Mills.
MUSCATINE, Iowa. Situated on the Mississippi River. Population, 8394.
Hotels—Eastern, Commercial, Scott.
MUSKEGON, Mich. Situated on Muskegon Lake, five miles from Lake Michigan. Population, 11,262. *Railroads*—Chicago & West Michigan. *Business interests*—Lumber (35 mills cut yearly 600,000,000 feet).
Hotels—Occidental, Hofstra.
NASHUA, N. H. Situated at the confluence of the Nashua and Merrimack Rivers. Population, 13,397. *Railroads*—Concord; Nashua, Acton & Boston; Nashua & Lowell—occupy separate depots; Nashua & Rochester; Worcester & Nashua—occupy same depot. *Business interests*—Manufacturing.
Hotels—Laton, Indian Head, Tremont.

For advertising space in this work address the National Directory Co., New York City.

NASHVILLE, Tenn. Situated on the Cumberland River. Population, 43,461. *Railroads*—Louisville & Nashville; Nashville, Chattanooga & St. Louis—occupy separate depots. *Business interests*—Mercantile, agricultural and manufacturing of furniture and agricultural implements.

Hotels—**Maxwell** ($3 per day), **Nicholson, Link's** (American plan, $2 per day ; European plan, rooms, 50c. and $1 per day), **Commercial.**

NEBRASKA CITY, Neb. Situated on the Missouri River. Population, 4800.

Hotels—**Grand Central, Barnum, Cincinnati.**

NEENAH, Wis. Situated on the Fox River, opposite Menasha, and near Lake Winnebago. Population, 4205.
Hotel—**Russell.**

NEGAUNEE, Mich. Population, 4005
Hotels—**Tilden, Breitung House**

NEW ALBANY, Ind. Situated on the Ohio River. Population, 16,422. *Railroads*—Jeffersonville, Madison & Indianapolis; Louisville, New Albany & Chicago; Louisville, Evansville & St. Louis—occupy separate depots. *Business interests*—Manufacturing and mercantile.
Hotels—**Central, Commercial, Gibson.**

NEWARK, N. J. Situated on the Passaic River, about four miles from its entrance into Newark Bay, nine miles from New York. Population, 136,400. *Railroads*— Delaware, Lackawanna & Western; New York, Lake Erie & Western; Pennsylvania (New York Division); Central of New Jersey (Newark and N. Y. Division)—

This work is circulated gratuitously among prominent hotels of the United States.

occupy separate depots. *Business interests*—Manufacturing and mercantile.

Hotels—Continental ($2 to $3 per day), **Park, Bristol.**

NEWARK, O. Situated at the confluence of the three forks of Licking River, and on the Ohio Canal. Population, 10,000. *Railroads*—Baltimore & Ohio (Central Ohio Division); Pittsburg, Cincinnati & St. Louis—occupy separate depots. *Business interests,*—Manufacturing, mercantile and agricultural.

Hotels—**Lansing, American, Park, Tubbs House.**

NEW BEDFORD, Mass. Situated on Buzzard Bay, at the mouth of Acushnet River. A port of entry. Population, 26,875. *Railroads*—Fall River; Old Colony—occupy same depot, *Business interests*—Commercial, mercantile, manufacturing and whaling.

Hotels—**Bancroft House, Mansion House, Parker House.**

NEWBERN, N. C. Situated at the confluence of Neuse and Trent Rivers. Population, 7000.

Hotels — **Central, Gaston, American, Farmer's Home, Henderson's, Palmer's.**

NEW BRIGHTON, Pa. Situated on the Beaver River. Population, 4214.

Hotels—**Keystone, Blount, Clyde, Sourbeck.**

NEW BRITAIN, Ct. Population, 13,937. *Railroads*—New York & New England; New York, New Haven & Hartford (Berlin branch). *Business interests*—Manufacturing.

Hotels—**City, Humphrey House, Strickland House.**

For advertising space in this work address the National Directory Co., New York City.

NEW BRUNSWICK, N. J. Situated on the Raritan River, at the Eastern terminus of the Delaware and Raritan Canal. Population, 17,167. *Railroads*—Pennsylvania. *Business interests*—Manufacturing, shipping and ship-building.

Hotels—**City, New Brunswick, White Hall, Bull's Head, Neilson House.**

NEWBURGH, N. Y. Situated on the Hudson River. Population, 18,050. *Railroads*—New York, West Shore & Buffalo; Ulster & Delaware—occupy same depot; New York, Lake Erie & Western (ferry connection with New York Central & Hudson River, and Newburgh, Dutchess & Connecticut; New York & New England)—separate depots. *Business interests*—Manufacturing.

Hotels—**Baldwin House, United States** ($2.50 per day), **Odell** (on European plan).

NEWBURYPORT, Mass. Situated on the Merrimac River. A port of entry. Population, 13,537. *Railroads*—Boston & Maine; Eastern—occupy separate depots. *Business interests*—Commercial, manufacturing and ship-building.

Hotels—**Merrimack, Ocean, American, City.**

NEWCASTLE, Pa. Situated on the Shenango and Neshannock Rivers. Population, 10,292. *Railroads*—Erie & Pittsburg; Chicago & Oil City; Pittsburg, Fort Wayne & Chicago—occupy same depot; Pittsburg & Lake Erie—occupies separate depot. *Business interests*—Manufacturing iron, nails, glass, mining limestone and coal, flouring mills, &c.

Hotels—**Leslie, Cochran, Crawford House.**

NEW HAVEN, Ct. Situated at the head of New

This work is circulated gratuitously among prominent hotels of the United States.

ESTERBROOK'S
Standard and Superior
STEEL ✺ PENS

FORGING THE PEN.

Leading Numbers. — *048, 14, 130, 333, 161.*

FOR SALE BY ALL STATIONERS.

THE ESTERBROOK STEEL PEN CO.,

Works, Camden, N. J   **26 John St., N. Y.**

❋MERIDEN❋
TURKISH BATH.

Turkish, Roman, Sulphur, Plain and Swimming Baths.

Pronounced by all travelers to be the finest equipped Bath-Rooms in the State. Open to gentlemen every day except Thursday from 9 a. m. until 9 p. m. Saturdays from 9 a.m until 12 p. m. Sunday, from 7 to 12 a. m.

Thursdays for Ladies, from 9 a. m. to 7 p. m.

❋ PRICES ❋

Turkish or Roman, 75c.; Sulphur, $1.00; Plain, 35c.
Swimming, - - 50 cents.

HARRY D. ALLEN, Proprietor,

Palace Block Annex,   MERIDEN, CONN.

Entrance on Hanover Street.

Haven Bay, four miles from its entrance into Long Island Sound. A port of entry. Population, 62,882. *Railroads*—Boston & New York Air-Line; New Haven & Northampton; New York, New Haven & Hartford; Shore Line—occupy same depot; New Haven & Derby—occupies separate depot. *Business interests*—Manufacturing, mercantile and commercial.

Hotels —**Elliott House** ($3 to $3.50 per day), **New Haven** ($4 per day), **Durant** ($2.50 per day), **Franklin House** ($1.50 per day), **Selden House** ($2 per day), **Grand Union** ($3 per day), **Union House** ($2 per day), **Tontine** ($2.50 to $3 per day), **Vischer's Hotel Yale** ($2 per day), **Tremont, The Woolsey.**

NEW LONDON, Ct. Situated on the Thames River, three miles from the ocean. Population, 10,529. *Railroads*—Central Vermont; New London Northern; New York, New Haven & Hartford; New York, Providence & Boston—all roads occupy same depot. Connected with New York by steamboat—two each night. *Business interests*—Commercial, mercantile, manufacturing, whaling and sealing.

Hotels — **Crocker, Metropolitan, Belden, Edgecomb, National, Pequot.**

NEW ORLEANS, La. Situated on the Mississippi River, between the river and Lake Ponchartrain, 110 miles from the Gulf of Mexico. Population, 216,140. *Railroads*—Chicago, St. Louis & New Orleans; Morgan's, Louisiana & Texas; New Orleans & Mobile; New Orleans & Northeastern—all roads occupy separate depots. *Business interests*—Commercial.

For advertising space in this work address the National Directory Co., New York City.

Hotels—**St. Charles** ($4 per day), **City** ($2.50 per day), **Cassidy's** ($2.50 per day), **St. James** ($2.50).

NEWPORT, R. I. Situated on Narragansett Bay. A port of entry. Population, 15,603. *Railroads*—Old Colony. *Business interests*—Manufacturing.

Hotels—**Ocean, Aquidneck, Perry, United States.**

NEW YORK CITY, N. Y. The chief city of the United States and the Western Continent, is located at the mouth of the Hudson River, in the southern part of the State of New York. The City Hall is in latitude 40° 42′ 43″ N., longitude 74° 0′ 3″ W., and the city occupies the county of the same name. It covers the whole of Manhattan Island and a portion of the mainland, and is bounded on the south by New York Bay; on the west by the Hudson or North River; on the north by the city of Yonkers and Westchester County, N. Y.; on the east by the river Bronx, that separates it from Westchester County, and the East River, a narrow, salt-water strait, dividing it from Long Island. It also includes Randall's, Ward's and Blackwell's Islands, in the East River; and Governor's Island, occupied by the U. S. Government; Bedloe's and Ellis' Islands, in the Bay. Spuyten Duyvil Creek and Harlem River divide the city into two unequal portions, and make the northern boundary of Manhattan Island. The city is 16 miles long, and varies in width from a few hundred yards to 4¼ miles at the north part. Its area is about 41½ square miles, or 26,500 acres, of which 12,100 are on the mainland. Its location is both beautiful, healthful, and advantageous in a commercial sense. Its commodious bay, the Hudson River, the neighboring sea, and the diversified country about it, contri-

---

This work is circulated gratuitously among prominent hotels of the United States.

—EASTERN—
FREIGHT CLAIM BUREAU,
234 BROADWAY,

Rooms 9, 10, 11 and 12. **New York.**

We make a Specialty of Settling Merchants' and Shippers' Claims of all kinds Loss and Damage, Overcharge, Rebates, etc., with Railroad, Transportation or Steamship Companies.

Claims are carried by us until vouchers are ready.

All Payments are made by the Companies direct to Claimants.

Our facilities as Experts enable us to secure speedy adjustments. Firms giving us entire charge of their claims are benefitted thereby, at about half the expense of any other system.

Matters pertaining to Special Rates, etc., strictly confidential. Rates—by the year, from $10 to $250 per month.

On commission, 10 per cent.

We respectfully solicit your business, guaranteeing satisfaction.

A representative will call on request.

ALFRED POST, Manager.

J. W. WHITE, General Eastern Agent.

Boston Office, 4 Exchange Place ; W. F. Stratton, New Eng. Agt.

Chicago Office, 177 La Salle St.: W. F. Hall.

BRAMHALL, DEANE & CO.

MANUFACTURERS OF DEANE'S PATENT

French Ranges and Broilers,

CARVING TABLES,

Coffee and Tea Urns, &c.

Nos. 274 and 282 FRONT STREET,

New York.

DIRECTLY UNDER N. Y. AND BROOKLYN BRIDGE.

Nos. 81 and 83 MARKET STREET, Chicago, Ills.

Cooking Utensils of Every Description.

bute to its attractiveness, while its varied surface and extensive water front conduce to its general healthfulness. Its harbor gives ample and safe anchorage for large fleets, and opens directly upon the Atlantic. Its position in the center of the northern part of the coast makes it a natural entrepôt for the Middle States; and the Hudson River, navigable for nearly 150 miles, places it in easy communication with the interior. The Erie Canal and several lines of railroads place the city in reach of the Great West, and on the east, New England almost joins the city. The State and City of New Jersey fringe the opposite bank of the Hudson, and along the East River the City of Brooklyn and its neighboring towns form a continuous city upon its eastern side. From the Battery, at the southern end of Manhattan Island, the view of the Bay, the Islands, Brooklyn Heights, Staten Island, the Jersey shore, Jersey City, and the entrance to the Hudson, presents one of the most animated and beautiful pictures to be found. The upper part of the city lies opposite the Palisades, and is remarkable for its rural and picturesque scenery. Its topography is at once favorable for business purposes and good drainage. The lower part of Manhattan Island, from the Battery north for about $3\frac{1}{2}$ miles, is rolling and sandy in character. It then rises slightly and becomes very rocky. At Central Park, near the center of the city, it rises into broken hills; and northward, along the river the land rises to a height of 238 feet at Washington Heights. Above the Island, the land is hilly and rough, with a great variety of scenery. The lower part of the city has been much altered by filling and grading, and the original width has been materially increased by filling in the rivers on both sides. The city

For advertising space in this work address the National Directory Co., New York City.

is compactly built up to the Harlem River, on the east of Central Park. This location is sometimes known as Harlem and Yorkville, being the sites of those villages. North of Harlem River are Mott Haven, Morrisania, West Farms, North New York, Port Morris, Woodstock, Highbridgeville, Claremont, Tremont, Mount Hope, Mount Eden, Fairmount, Belmont, Fordham, and Williamsbridge. West of Central Park the population centers in the villages of Bloomingdale and Manhattanville. North of these, along the Hudson, are Washington Heights, Inwood, Kingsbridge, Spuyten Duyvil, Mosholu, Riverdale, and Mount St. Vincent. All of these places are now included in New York City. The ways of approach to New York are numerous, since it is in communication with all parts of the globe, either by sea or railroad. From the sea it is approached from the south by Sandy Hook through the Narrows, between Long Island on the east, and Staten Island on the west, into New York Bay, passing the great fortresses of Fort Tompkins and Fort Richmond on the west, or Staten Island shore and Fort Hamilton on the east, or Long Island shore, while old Fort Lafayette, of the "Great Rebellion" celebrity, stands in the bay, a short distance from the shore. At the confluence of the East and Hudson Rivers is Governor's Island, distinguished by the circular fortress on its northern shore. The Hamburg and German lines of steamers land their passengers at Hoboken; while the Cunard, Inman, White Star, Anchor, National and French lines discharge theirs at different piers on the Hudson River, or west side of the city. There is another channel of approach from the sea through the Kills, between Staten Island, on the New

---

This work is circulated gratuitously among prominent hotels of the United States.

Jersey shore, connecting Raritan Bay with New York Harbor—but only vessels of light draught can approach by this route. Steamers and vessels approaching from Long Island Sound pass through Hell Gate and discharge cargoes on both the East River and North River piers. The Hartford, New Haven, Bridgeport, and other steamboats from nearer ports, land at East River piers—at Peck slip and vicinity ; while the Fall River, Stonington, Providence, Norwich and New London, and Boston outside lines, pass round the Battery and discharge at North or Hudson River piers. The Hudson River steamboats all discharge on the west, or North River side of the city. Passengers via New York and New Haven, Harlem, New York Central and Hudson River Railroads, are dropped at the Grand Central Depot, East 42d Street and Fourth Avenue. All railroad passengers from Boston and the East are landed at Grand Central Depot. The Pennsylvania Railroad lands its passengers by ferry-boat, from Jersey City, at Cortlandt Street and Desbrosses Street. The N. Y. West Shore and Buffalo at W. 39th Street, and at Cortlandt and Desbrosses Streets; and the N. Y., Susquehanna and Western at Chambers Street and W. 23d Street. The Erie Railroad and Northern New Jersey by ferry to Chambers Street and W. 23d Street. Central New Jersey by ferry to Liberty Street. Delaware, Lackawanna and Western by ferry to Barclay and Christopher Streets. Staten Island by ferry to Whitehall, and Long Island by ferry to Roosevelt and E. 34th Streets. *Railroads*—Baltimore & Ohio—depot, foot of Cortlandt Street and foot of Desbrosses Street ; Central of New Jersey—depot, foot of Liberty Street ; Delaware, Lackawanna & Western—depot, Hoboken ferries, Barclay and

For advertising space in this work address the National Directory Co., New York City.

Christopher Streets; Erie Railway—depot, pier 30, foot of Chambers Street and W. 23d Street ferry; Hackensack & New York—foot chamber Street and W. 23d Street ferry; Lehigh Valley Railway—depot, foot of Cortlandt and Desbrosses Streets ; Long Island R. R —depot, James' Slip and E. 34th Street ; Manhattan Beach Railway—foot of James Slip, E. 34th Street and Whitehall Street; Morris and Essex—foot Barclay and Christopher Streets ; N. J. Southern—foot of Murray Street, direct route to Long Branch ; N. J. Midland—depot, foot of Cortlandt Street, Jersey City ferries; New York Central & Hudson River—Grand Central Depot, 42th Street and 4th Avenue; New York & Boston , New York & Harlem ; New York & New Haven—same depot, 4th Avenue and 42d Street ; New York City & Northern Railway—depot, 155th Street and 8th Avenue; New York, Ontario & Western Railway; New York, West Shore & Buffalo Railway—same depots, foot of Cortland Street, foot of Desbrosses Street, and foot of W. 42d Street; Northern New Jersey—depots, foot of Chambers and West 23d Streets ; Pennsylvania Railroad —depot, foot of Cortlandt Street and foot of Desbrosses Street. *Steamboats*—Caution.—Frequent changes are made in the running time of the various steamboats in this list. Consult the daily papers. Albany—Catskill, Newburgh, West Point and points along the river : Albany Day Line from pier 39 N. R., at 8.35 a. m., and foot of W. 22d Street, at 9 a. m. People's Line from pier 41, N. R., at 6 p. m. to Albany only ; Bridgeport—Bridgeport Steamboat Co., from pier 35, E. R., at 11 a. m. and 3 p. m. Steamer Rosedale from pier 25, E. R., at 3 p. m.; Boston—Fall River Line, from pier 28, N. R., summer, 5 p. m., winter, 4 p. m.; Norwich Line, from pier 40, N. R., summer, 5 p. m.,

This work is circulated gratuitously among prominent hotels of the United States.

winter, 4 p. m.; Providence Line, from pier 29, N. R., summer, 5 p. m., winter, 4 p. m.; Stonington Line, from pier 33, N. R., summer, 5 p. m., winter, 4 p. m.; Catskill —Catskill Line of Steamers, from pier 34, N. R., at 6 p. m.; and regular Hudson River Day Line Steamers, from pier 39. N. R.; Fall River—Fall River Line, from pier 28. N. R., summer, 5 p. m., winter, 4 p. m.; Greenport—Sag Harbor and Shelter Island, Steamer W. W. Coit, from pier 25, E. R., Tuesday, Thursday, Saturday, 5 p. m.; Hudson—Steamers McManus and Redfield, from pier 35, N. R., at 6 p. m., and Hudson River "Day Line" of Steamers, from pier 39, N. R.; Long Branch—Steamer from pier 8, N. R., 4.30, 10.15 a. m., 3.45, 4.45 p. m.; Hartford, Middletown, and points on Connecticut River, from pier 25, E. R., at 4 p. m.; New Haven (only) —New Haven Boat, from pier 26, E. R., 3 p. m.; Starin's Line, from pier 18, N. R., 9 p. m.; New London—Norwich Line Steamers, from pier 40, N. R., 5 p m.; Newport—Newport Line Steamers, from pier 28, N. R., 5 p. m.; Norwich—Norwich Line Steamers, from pier 40, N. R., 5 p. m.; Nyack and points along the river —Steamer Chrystenah, from pier 44, N. R., 3.30 p. m.; Poughkeepsie—Steamer Mary Powell, 3.15 p. m., from pier 39, N. R., and 3.30 p. m., from foot of W. 22d Street; also "Day Line" Steamers, from pier 39, N. R., 8.35 a. m.; Providence—Providence Line, from pier 29, N. R., 5 p.m, in summer, and 4 p. m. in winter; Rondout and Kingston—Steamer Mary Powell, from pier 39, N. R., 3.15 p.m., foot W. 22d Street, 3.30 p. m.; also steamer from pier 34, N. R., 4 p. m.; Stonington—Stonington Line, from pier 33, N. R., 5 p. m. in summer, and 4 p. m. in winter; Troy —Citizen's Line, from pier 44, N. R., 6 p. m., and Al-

For advertising space in this work address the National Directory Co., New York City.

bany Day Line from pier 39, N. R., 8.35 a. m., and foot W. 22d Street at 9 a. m.; West Point—Albany Day Line Steamers, pier 39, N. R., 8.35 a. m., and foot W. 22d Street, 9 a. m.; also Steamer Mary Powell, from pier 39 N. R., 3.15 p. m., and foot W. 22d Street, 9.30 a. m. *Ocean Steamers—Foreign Ports*—(M. monthly, S. M. semi-monthly, T. M. tri-monthly, W. weekly, S. W. semi-weekly, T. W. tri-weekly, D. daily.) Amsterdam—S. M., Sussex Street pier, Jersey City, office, Funch, Edye & Co., 27 William Street; Antwerp—S. M., Grand Street pier, Jersey City, office, Red Star Line, 55 Broadway; Aspinwall—S. M., new pier 34, N. R., office, Pacific Mail S. S. Co., new pier 34; Bermuda—S. M., pier 52, N. R., office, A. E. Outerbridge, 51 Broadway; Brazil and Porto Rico—M., Robert's Dock, Brooklyn, office, P. F. Gerhart & Co., 19 S. William Street; Bremen, via Southampton—W., Third Street pier, Hoboken, office, Oelrichs & Co., 2 Bowling Green; Bristol, England —S. M., pier 18, E. R., office, W. D. Morgan, 70 South Street; China & Japan, via San Francisco—S. M., new pier 34, N. R , office, Pacific Mail S. S. Co., new pier 34; Glasgow, via Londonderry—W., pier 20, N. R., office, Anchor Line, 7 Bowling Green ; Glasgow, via Belfast— W., New pier 34, N. R. office, Austin, Baldwin & Co., 53 Broadway; Halifax, N. S.—office, Lord & Austin, 9 Beaver street; Hamburg, via Plymouth and Cherbourg— W., Third Street pier, Hoboken, office, C. B. Richards & Co., 61 Broadway ; Havana & Mexico—T. M., pier 3, N. R., office, F. Alexander & Sons, 33 Broadway ; Havana— T. M., pier 16, E. R , office, Jas. E. Ward & Co., 113 Wall Street; Havre & Brest. via Plymouth—pier 42, N. R., office, Louis de Bebian, 6 Bowling Green ; Hayti, Jamaica

---

This work is circulated gratuitously among prominent hotels of the United States.

& New Grenada—S. M., pier foot of W. 25th Street, office, Pim, Forwood & Co., 21 State Street; Hull, via Southampton—S. M., office, Sanderson & Son, 39 S. William Street; Liverpool, via Queenstown —W., new pier 40, N. R., office, Cunard Line, 4 Bowling Green; Liverpool, via Queenstown—W., new pier 37, N. R., office, Inman Line, 31 Broadway; Liverpool, via Queenstown—W., pier 42, N. R., office, White Star Line, 37 Broadway; Liverpool, via Queenstown—W., new pier 9, N. R., office, National Line, 69 Broadway; Liverpool, via Queenstown—W., new pier 38, N. R., office, Guion & Co., 29 Broadway; Liverpool, via Queenstown—S. M., pier 53, N. R.; office, Anchor Line, 7 Bowling Green; London—M., new pier 39, N. R., office, F. W. J. Hurst, 69 Broadway; London—W. Pavonia Ferry pier, N. J., office, Patton, Vickers & Co., 35 Broadway; London, Bordeaux & Mediterranean—S. M., pier 53, N. R., office, Anchor Line, 7 Bowling Green; Nassau—M., pier 17 E. R., office, Jas. E. Ward & Co., 113 Wall Street; St. Domingo & Samana —office, W. P. Clyde & Co., 35 Broadway; St. Johns, N. F.—office, Bowing & Archibald, 39 Broadway; St. Thomas & Venezuela—Robert's Dock, Brooklyn, office, P. F. Gerhard & Co., 19 S. William Street. *Domestic Ports*—Alexandria, Va., & Washington, D. C.—W., pier 41 E. R., office, T. W. Wightman, 241 South Street; Charleston, S. C.—S. W., pier 27 N. R., office, W. H. Rhett, 317 Broadway; Fernandina, Fla., & Port Royal, S. C.—W., pier 20, N. R., office, C. H. Mallory & Co., pier 20, E. R.; Galveston, Texas, via Key West—W., pier 20 E. R., office, C. H. Mallory & Co., pier 20 E. R. New Orleans—W., pier 36 N. R., office, Morgan's Line, pier 36, N. R.; New Orleans—W., pier 9, E. R., office,

---

For advertising space in this work address the National Directory Co., New York City.

Samuel H. Seaman, pier 9, N. R.; Philadelphia—D., pier 33, E. R., office, W. P. Clyde & Co., pier 33, E. R.; Portland, Me.—S. W., pier 38 E. R., office, J. F. Ames, pier 38 E. R., Richmond, Portsmouth, Norfolk & City Point, Va., & Lewes, Del.—T. W., pier 37, N. R., office, Old Dominion Line, 235 West Street; San Francisco, via Panama—S. M., new pier 34, N. R., office, Pacific Mail S. S. Co., new pier 34; Savannah, Ga.—S. W., pier 43, N. R., office, W. H. Rhett, Agent, 317 Broadway; Wilmington, Del.—T. W., pier 14, E. R., office, Abiel Abbot, 53 South Street; Wilmington, N. C.—W., pier 34 & 35, E. R., office, W. P. Clyde & Co., 35 Broadway.

Hotels—**Cosmopolitan**, cor. Chambers Street & West Broadway, ($1.00 and up per day), N. & S. J. Huggins, props.; **Albemarle**, Broadway, 5th Avenue & 24th Street, ($2.00 and up per day), L. H. Janvrin & Co., props.; **Grand**, Broadway, cor. 31st Street, ($1.50 and up per day), Henry Milford Smith & Son, props.; **Gedney House**, 40th Street & Broadway, ($1.00 and up, per day). Bowers Bros., props.; **Normandie**, Broadway, cor. 38th Street, ($2.00 and up per day), Ferdinand P. Earle, prop.; **Fifth Avenue**, Madison Square, ($5.00 per day); **St. Cloud**, Broadway & 42d Street, ($1.00 and up per day), Rand Bros., props.; **St. James**, Broadway & 26th Street, (S. Rooms, $2.00 & $2.50, D. Rooms, $3.00, $4.00 to $6.00), Wm. M. Conner, prop.; **Barrett House**, Broadway, cor. 43d Street, ($1.50 and up per day), Barrett, Bros. prop.; **Sturtevant House**, Broadway, 28th & 29th Streets, (American Plan, $2.50 and up per day), L. & T. S. Leland, props.; **Coleman House**, Broadway & 27th Street, ($1.00 and up per day), Jas. H. Rodgers, prop.; **Brighton**, Broadway, 42d Street & 7th Avenue, ($1.00 and up per

---

This work is circulated gratuitously among prominent hotels of the United States.

day), Albert A. Durand, prop.; **Union Square,** Union Square, cor. 15th Street, A. J. Dam & Son, prop.; **Astor House,** Broadway, cor. Barclay Street, ($1.00 to $5.00 per day), Allen & Dam, props., F. T. Keith, manager; **Madison,** Broadway & 39th Street, ($2 00 and up per day), Wm. C. Kitsell, prop.; **Rossmore,** Broadway, 41st & 42d Streets, ($3.00 to $3.50 per day, Rooms, $1.00 and up per day), Temple & Putney, props.; **Everett House,** Union Square, 4th Avenue, cor. 18th Street, $1.00 to $5.00 per day), C. H. Kerney, prop.; **Continental,** 20th Street & Broadway, ($1.00 to $5.00 per day), E. L. Merrifield, prop.; **St. Denis Hotel & Taylor's Saloon,** Broadway & 11th Street, ($1.00 and up per day), William Taylor, prop.; **Brunswick,** 5th Avenue, ($1 to $5 per day), Mitchell & Kinzler, props.; **Gilsey House,** Broadway & 29th Street, ($2 and up per day), J. H. Breslin & Bro., props.; **Hoffman House,** Madison Square, ($2 and up per day), C. H. Read & Co., props.; **Ashland House,** 24th Street & 4th Avenue, (American Plan, $2 to $3 per day, Rooms, $1 and up per day), H. H. Brockway, prop.; **Morton House,** Broadway & 14th Street, ($1 and up per day), C. E. Vernum, prop.; **Grand Central,** 667 to 677 Broadway, op. Bond Street, (Full Board, $3 to $3.50 per day, Rooms, $1 and up per day), Keefer & Co., props.; **Metropolitan,** Broadway & Prince St., (Full Board, $3 per day), Henry Clair, lessee; **Sinclair House,** Broadway, cor. 8th Street, ($1 to $3 per day), A. L. Ashman & Son, props.; **New York Hotel,** Broadway, Washington & Waverly Place, (Full Board, $3.50 per day), H. Cranston, prop.; **Belmont,** 137 Fulton Street; **Belvedere,** 4th Avenue & 18th Street; **Brevoort House,** 11 5th Avenue; **Bristol,** 5th Avenue &

For advertising space in this work address the National Directory Co., New York City.

42d Street; **Broadway**, 834 Broadway; **Brower House**, Broadway, cor. 28th Street; **Buckingham**, 5th Avenue & 50th Street; **Canda House**, Lafayette Place, near 4th Street; **Clarendon**, 4th Avenue, cor. 18th Street; **Colonade**, 726 Broadway; **Commercial**, Broadway & Washington Place; **Everett's**, 84 Chatham Street; **Earle's**, Canal & Centre Streets; **Frankenstein's**, 413 Broome Street; **Glenham**, 155 5th Avenue, **Grand Union**, 4th Avenue & 42d Street; **Hall's**, Chambers & Chatham Streets; **Branting**, Madison Avenue, cor. 58th Street; **Dam**, 15th Street, near 4th Avenue; **Devonshire**, 30 East 42d Street; **Espanol**, 116 & 118 West 14th Street; **Recreo**, 15th Street, cor. Irving Place; **Royal**, 6th Avenue & 40th Street; **Shelburn**, 5th Avenue, cor. 36 Street; **St. Marc**, 5th Avenue, cor. 38th Street; **St. Stephen**, 34 W. 11th Street, **International**, 17 & 19 Park Row; **Irving House**, Broadway, cor. 12th Street; **Leggett's**, 44 Chatham Street; **Leland**, Broadway & 27th Street; **Manhattan**, Broadway, cor. Canal Street; **Merchant's**, 39 Cortlandt Street; **Occidental**, Broome Street & Bowery; **Park Avenue**, 4th Avenue & 32d Street; **Prescott House**, Broadway & Spring Street; **Revere House**, Broadway, cor. Houston Street; **St. Nicholas**, 515 Broadway; **St. Omer**, 384 & 386 6th Avenue; **Stevens House**, 23 Broadway; **Sweeney's**, Chambers & Chatham Streets; **Tremont House**, 665 Broadway; **United States**, Fulton & Water Streets; **Vanderbilt**, Lexington Avenue & 42d Street; **Victoria**, Broadway, 27th & 5th Avenue; **Westminster**, Irving Place & 16th Street; **Windsor**, 5th Avenue & 46th Street.

NEWPORT, Ark. Situated upon the St. Louis Iron Mountain R'y, where it crosses the White River, to which point steamboats navigate. Population, 750.

This work is circulated gratuitously among prominent hotels of the United States.

Hotels—Lucas, Horton and Railroad.

NEWTON, Kansas. Population, 5000.
Hotels—Arcade, Howard House.

NIAGARA FALLS, N. Y. Situated at the Falls of Niagara River, twenty miles north of Buffalo, and fourteen miles south of Lake Ontario. Population, 5,048 The cataract of Niagara has a perpendicular fall of one hundred and sixty-five feet. The rapids commence about three-fourths of a mile above the main fall. Goat Island, a quarter of a mile wide, and half a mile long, extends to the very brow of the precipice and divides the falls into two portions, the higher of which is on the American side, but the greater body of water is on the Canadian. Below the falls the river runs between perpendicular cliffs for three or four miles, in a channel of from three to eight hundred feet in width, forming the whirlpool and lower rapids.

Hotels—On the American side, Cataract, International, Spencer, Niagara, Kaltenbath Pacific ; on the Canada side, Clifton, Prospect, Brunswick.

NILES, Mich. Situated on the St. Joseph River. Population, 4500.
Hotels—Bond, Pike, Farler.

NORFOLK, Va. A port of entry. Situated at the mouth of the Elizabeth River and the Dismal Swamp Canal, by which connection is made with Albemarle Sound. Opposite Portsmouth, Va. Population, 21,966. *Railroads*—Atlantic, Mississippi & Ohio; Norfolk Southern ; Norfolk & Virginia Beach ; Norfolk & Ocean View. *Business interests*—Those connected with cotton and shipping of oysters, fish, vegetables, fruit, &c.

For advertising space in this work address the National Directory Co., New York City.

Hotels—Atlantic, **Purcell House** ($2.50, $3, and $3.50).

NORRISTOWN, Pa. Situated on the Schuylkill River. Population, 13,064. *Railroad*—Philadelphia & Reading. *Business interests*—Manufacturing and mercantile.

Hotels—**Verandah, Rambo, Farmers', Montgomery House, Windsor House.**

NORTH ADAMS, Mass. Population, 10,192. *Railroads*—Boston & Albany ; Fitchburg ; Troy & Boston ; New Haven & Northampton ; Boston, Hoosac Tunnel & Western—occupy same depot. *Business interests*—Manufacturing.

Hotels—**Richmond House, Ballou, Wilson.**

NORTHAMPTON, Mass. Situated on the Connecticut River. Population, 12,172. *Railroads*—Connecticut River ; New Haven & Northampton—occupy separate depots. *Business interests*—Mercantile and extensive manufacturers of silk, paper, cutlery, cotton, buttons, tape, &c.

Hotels—**Mansion, Round Hill** (a summer hotel), **Hampshire, Nonotuck.**

NORWALK, Ct. Situated on both sides of the Norwalk River, near its entrance into Long Island Sound. Population, 13,956. *Railroads*—Danbury & Norwalk. *Business interests*—Manufacturing and mercantile.

Hotels—**Connecticut, Norwalk, Adams.**

NORWALK, O. Population, 5831.
Hotels—**St. Charles, Weber, Baldwin.**

This work is circulated gratuitously among prominent hotels of the United States.

NORWICH, N. Y. Situated on the Chenango River and Canal. Population, 5,000.
Hotels--Eagle, American, Palmer, Spaulding.

NORWICH, Ct. Situated on the Thames River, at the mouth of the Yantic River. Population, 21,141. *Railroads*—New York & New England, Norwich Division; New London & Northern—occupy separate depots. *Business interests*--Manufacturing.
Hotels--Wauregan, American, Metropolitan, Union Square.

OAKLAND, Cal. Situated on San Francisco Bay; connected by ferry with San Francisco. Population, 34,556. *Railroads*—Central Pacific ; South Pacific Coast—occupy separate depots.
Hotels Newland, Centennial, Galindo, Winsor, Hartman, Roberts, Tubbs, Kohler, Chase.

OBERLIN, O. Population, 3242.
Hotel--Park House.

OGDEN, Utah. Situated at the junction of the Weber and Ogden Rivers, and at the mouth of the Ogden Canyon, one of the gorges which pierce the Wahsatch range. Population, 5313. The Union and Central Pacific roads have here machine and repair shops, round-houses, etc.
Hotels—Union, Junction, Globe City.

OGDENSBURG, N. Y. Situated on the St. Lawrence River, at the mouth of the Oswegatchie River, opposite Prescott, Can., and connected by ferry. Population, 10,340. *Railroads*—Ogdensburg & Lake Champlain; Rome, Watertown & Ogdensburg; Utica & Black River—occupy separate depots. *Business interests*—Manufactur-

---

For advertising space in this work address the National Directory Co., New York City.

ing and commercial. Here are large elevators and warehouses for the transhipment of grain.
Hotels—**Windsor, Seymour, Johnson, Commercial, National.**

OIL CITY, Pa. Situated at the confluence of Oil Creek and the Allegheny River. Population, 9644. This city is the centre of the oil trade of this region.
Hotels—**Collins, National, Taylor.**

OLD POINT COMFORT, Va. Situated at the confluence of the Chesapeake Bay and Hampton Roads, about 180 miles south of Baltimore, Md., and 15 miles north of Norfolk and Portsmouth, Va. Site of Fortress Monroe, largest fortification in the United States. Celebrated as a health and pleasure resort.
Hotel—**Hygeia.**

OLYMPIA, Washington Ter. Located on Puget Sound and is reached by steamers, and is the northern terminus of the Olympia & Chehalis Valley R. R., connecting with the Northern Pacific R'y at Tenis Station. *Business interest*—Mercantile.
Hotels—**Carlton, Pacific, New England, St. Charles.**

OMAHA, Neb. Situated on the Missouri River. Population, 30,518. *Railroads*—Burlington & Missouri River in Nebraska; Union Pacific; Omaha & Northern Nebraska; Chicago, St. Paul, Minneapolis & Omaha; Missouri Pacific—occupy separate depots. (For additional roads see Council Bluffs, Ia.) *Business interests*—Commercial, mercantile and manufacturing, extensive smelting and refining works, &c. *Banks*—The Nebraska National. During the season of navigation steamers run to

This work is circulated gratuitously among prominent hotels of the United States.

St. Louis and Upper Missouri and Yellowstone River points.
Hotels—Millard ($3 to $4 per day), Cozzens ($2 per day), Paxton ($3 and $4 per day), Metropolitan.

ONEIDA, N. Y. Population, 3932. A community of about 300 men and women, residing in large buildings on a fruitful farm two miles south of the Central Railway station, is known as the Oneida Community.
Hotel—Allen.

ONEONTA, N. Y. Situated on the Susquehanna River, and Delaware & Hudson Canal Co.'s R. R. Population, 3004.
Hotels—Central, Susquehanna, Haathway House.

OPELIKA, Ala. Population, 3330.
Hotels—Opelika, Melton.

ORANGE, N. J. Population, 13.206. *Railroads*—Delaware, Lackawanna & Western (Morris & Essex Div.); New York & Greenwood Lake. *Business interests*—Manufacturing.
Hotels—City, Park, Central, Mansion, Hang's.

OSAGE CITY, Kan. Population, 2158.
Hotels—Palace, Osage.

OSKALOOSA, Ia. Population, 4800.
Hotels—Downing House, Burnett House.

OSHKOSH, Wis. Situated on Lake Winnebago, at the mouth of Fox River. Population, 15,749. *Railroads*—Chicago & Northwestern; Chicago, Milwaukee & St. Paul; Wisconsin Central; Milwaukee, Lake Shore & Western—occupy separate depots. *Business interests*—Lumber, carriages, trunks, sash, doors and blinds.

For advertising space in this work address the National Directory Co., New York City.

Hotels—**Tremont, Revere, Seymour.**

OSWEGO, N. Y. Situated on Lake Ontario, at the mouth of the Oswego River—it is also the northern terminus of the Oswego Canal. Population, 21,117. *Railroads*—Delaware, Lackawanna & Western—depot on Utica Street, in Lake Shore Hotel Block; Rome, Watertown & Ogdensburg; New York, Ontario & Western—Occupy separate depots. *Business interests*—Manufacturing, starch, flour, shipping, commission business, &c.

Hotels—**Hamilton, Lake Shore, Doolittle House,** at which are the celebrated Deep Rock Springs.

OTTAWA, Ill. Situated on the Illinois River and Illinois and Michigan Canal. Population, 10,000. *Railroads*—Chicago, Burlington & Quincy; Chicago, Rock Island & Pacific—occupy separate depots. *Business interests*—Agricultural and manufacturing, extensive window glass, bottle and starch factories, also tile, fire-brick, flour, &c.

Hotels—**Clifton, White, St. Nicholas, Ottawa.**

OTTAWA, Ont. Situated on the Ottawa River and Rideau Canal. Population, 25,000. *Railroads*—Canada Central; St. Lawrence & Ottawa; Quebec, Montreal, Ottawa & Occidental—occupy separate depots. *Business interests*—Lumber.

Hotels—**St. Lawrence, Windsor, Albion, Russell House, Union House.**

OTTUMWA, Ia. Situated on the Des Moines River. Population, 9018.

Hotels—**Ballingall, Revere, Baker** ($2 per day).

OWATONNA, Minn. Situated on the Straight River. Population, 3200.

This work is circulated gratuitously among prominent hotels of the United States.

Hotels—Arnold, Winship, Parker, Nickerson, Morehouse.

OWEGO, N. Y. Situated on the Susquehanna River. Population, 6037.
Hotels—United States, Park, Ah-wa-sa ($2 per day), Central, Cortright, Exchange.

OWENSBORO, Ky. Situated on the Ohio River, 155 miles by water, below Louisville, Ky. Population, 10,000. *Railroad*—Owensboro & Nashville. *Business interest*—Manufacturing.
Hotels—Planters', Brooks, McCullough.

PADUCAH, Ky. Situated on the Ohio River at the mouth of the Tennessee River, fifty miles above Cairo. Population, 10,868. *Railroads*—Memphis, Paducah & Northern; Paducah & Elizabethtown—occupy joint depot. *Business interests*—Manufacturing and mercantile.
Hotels—Richmond, Maxwell, Southern, Planters'.

PAINESVILLE, O. Situated on Grand River, three miles from Lake Erie. Population, 3850.
Hotels—Stockwell House, Cowles House.

PALESTINE, Tex. Population, 3500.
Hotels—La Clede, Hunter, Sterne.

PALMYRA, N. Y. Population, 3014.
Hotels—Palmyra, Cummings, Throp, Exchange.

PARSONS, Kansas. Situated on Missouri, Kansas & Texas Division of the Mo. Pacific R'y, 293 miles from Hannibal, Mo., and 338 miles from St. Louis. Population, 5000.
Hotels—Abbott, Southern, Worth.

PARKERSBURG, W. Va. Situated on the Ohio River

For advertising space in this work address the National Directory Co., New York City.

which is crossed by a magnificent railroad bridge. Population, 6510.

Hotels—**Swan, Hills Central.**

PASSAIC, N. J. Population, 7000.

Hotels—**City, Lyceum, Mansion.**

PATERSON, N. J. Situated on the Passaic River, immediately below the falls. Population, 50,887. *Railroads*—Delaware, Lackawanna & Western; New York, Lake Erie & Western; New Jersey Midland—occupy separate depots. *Business interests*—Rolling Mills, manufacturing locomotives, silk, cotton, etc.

Hotels—**Passaic, Franklin House, Hamilton House.**

PAWTUCKET, R. I. Situated on the Pawtucket River. Population, 19,030. *Railroads*—Boston & Providence; New York & New England; Providence & Worcester—occupy same depot. *Business interests*—Manufacturing and commercial.

Hotels—**Benedict, Pawtucket.**

PEABODY, Mass. Population, 9033.

Hotels—**Symond's, Baldwin, Donnell, Peabody.**

PEEKSKILL, N. Y. Situated on the left bank of the Hudson, 41 miles above N. Y. City and surrounded by the finest scenery on the river. It has a population of 6990.

Hotels—**Eagle, Exchange.**

PEKIN, Ill. Situated on the east bank of the Illinois River. Population, 6500.

Hotels—**Woodward's Hotel, Planters', Bemis.**

PENN YAN, N. Y. Situated at the foot of Lake Keuka. Population, 3497.

This work is circulated gratuitously among prominent hotels of the United States.

Hotels—Benham, Central, Knapp, Sherman.

PENSACOLA, Fla. Situated on Pensacola Bay, Population, 7600.
Hotels—City, Merchants.

PEORIA, Ill. Situated on the Illinois River. Population, 29,315. *Railroads*—Chicago, Burlington & Quincy; Illinois Midland; Indiana, Bloomington & Western; Peoria, Decatur & Evansville; Peoria & Pekin Union; Wabash, St. Louis & Pacific; Rock Island & Peoria—all occupy same depot; Chicago, Rock Island & Pacific—separate depot. *Business interests*—Mercantile and manufacturing.
Hotels—Peoria, White House, Merchants'.

PERTH AMBOY, N. J. Situated at Junction of Raritan Bay with Staten Island Sound. Population, 4808.
Hotels—Central, Packer.

PERU, Ind. Situated on the Wabash River and Wabash and Erie Canal. Population, 6000.
Hotels—St. James, American, National, Tremont, Bearos.

PETERSBOROUGH, Ont. Situated on the Otanabee River. Population, 7000.
Hotels—Hoffman, Casey House.

PETERSBURG, Va. Situated on the Appomattox River. Population, 21,656. *Railroads*—Norfolk & Western; Richmond & Petersburg—occupy separate depots; Richmond & Petersburg also occupies depot with Petersburg R. R. *Business interests*—Manufacturing (tobacco, sumac), mercantile and commercial.
Hotels—Bollingbrooke, Jarrett, Newton.

For advertising space in this work address the National Directory Co., New York City.

PHILADELPHIA, Pa. Situated between the rivers Delaware and Schuylkill. A port of entry. Population, 846,984. *Railroads*—Camden & Atlantic, foot of Vine St.; Camden, Gloucester & Mount Ephraim, foot of South St.; Pennsylvania—(N. Y. & Pennsylvania Divisions), Broad and Market Sts.; Kensington Depot, Front St. and Montgomery Ave., Amboy Division, foot of Market St., north side; Philadelphia, Newton & New York, 32d and Market Sts.; Philadelphia & Atlantic City, Pier 8, South Delaware Ave.; Philadelphia, Wilmington & Baltimore, and Philadelphia & Baltimore Central, Broad St. and Washington Ave., Philadelphia & Reading—Main Line, Broad and Collowhill Sts.; North Pennsylvania & Bound Brook Division, 3d and Berks Sts. and 9th and Green Sts.; Germantown and Norristown Branch, 9th and Green Sts.; West Chester & Philadelphia, 31st and Chestnut Sts.; West Jersey, Foot of Market St., north side. *Business interests*—Manufacturing, commercial, mercantile, etc. Second city in commercial importance and population in the United States. Office of the National Railway Publication Co., Nos. 229 and 231 South Fifth Street.

Hotels—**Aldine, American, Bellevue, Bingham, Continental, Colonnade, Girard, Guy's, Lafayette, St. Charles, St. Cloud, St. Elmo, St. George, Merchants', Washington,** etc.

PHILLIPSBURG, N. J. Situated on the Delaware River, opposite Easton, Pa., and terminus of the Morris Canal. Population, 7169.

Hotels—**Lee, Columbia, Phillipsburg, Union Square.**

PHŒNIXVILLE, Pa. Situated on the Schuylkill

This work is circulated gratuitously among prominent hotels of the United States.

River, at the mouth of French River; also, on the Schuylkill Canal. Population, 6692.
Hotels—**Phœnix, Washington, Mansion, Union.**

PIERCE CITY, Mo. Situated on the St. Louis & San Francisco R'y, 290 miles southwest of St. Louis. Population, 1300.
Hotels—**Decatur, Merchants'.**

PIQUA, O. Situated on the Miami River and Miami and Erie Canal. Population, 6036.
Hotels—**Leland, City.**

PITTSBURG, Pa. Situated at the confluence of the Allegheny and Monongahela Rivers, which form the Ohio. A port of entry. Population, 156,381. *Railroads* —Allegheny Valley; Cleveland & Pittsburg; Pennsylvania (Main Line, and Pittsburg, Virginia & Charleston Branch); Pittsburg, Cincinnati & St. Louis ; Pittsburg, Fort Wayne & Chicago—occupy same depot; Baltimore & Ohio ; Pennsylvania (West Penna. Div.); Pittsburg & Castle Shannon ; Pittsburg & Lake Erie ; Pittsburg Southern; Pittsburg & Western—occupy separate depots. *Business interests*—Manufacturing on the largest scale, principally of iron and glass; mercantile and commercial.
Hotels—**Monongahela, Seventh Avenue** ($2.50 and $3 per day), **St. Charles, Central.**

PITTSFIELD, Mass. Population, 13,367. *Railroads* —Boston & Albany ; Housatonic—occupy same depot. *Business interests*—Manufacturing.
Hotels—**American, Burbank, Berkshire.**

PITTSTON, Pa. Population, 10,005. *Railroads*—Central of New Jersey ; Delaware, Lackawanna & Western ;

For advertising space in this work address the National Directory Co., New York City.

Lehigh Valley—occupy separate depots. *Business interests*—Coal mining and manufacturing.
Hotels—**Eagle, Gething, St. James, Farnham House.**

PLAINFIELD, N. J. Population, 8005.
Hotels—**Laing's, Park House.**

PLATTSBURG, N. Y. Population, 5600. Situated on both sides of the Saranac River, at its entrance into Cumberland Bay, of Lake Champlain.
Hotels—**Cumberland House, Fouquet House, Witherill House.**

PLYMOUTH, Ind. Situated on Yellow River. Population, 2800.
Hotels—**Ross, Parker, Vernedge.**

PLYMOUTH, Mass. Situated on Plymouth Bay. Population, 7094.
Hotels—**Brastow, Central, Clifford, Franklin, Manomet, Plymouth Rock, Samoset.**

PORTAGE CITY, Wis. Situated on the Wisconsin River. Population, 4446.
Hotels—**City, Emder's, Corning House ($2 per day), Fox House, Kirby House.**

PORT HOPE, Ont. Situated on Lake Ontario. Population, 6000.
Hotels—**Queen's, St. Lawrence Hall.**

PORT HURON, Mich. Situated on the St. Clair River, at the mouth of Black River, one mile from Lake Huron. Population, 10,000. *Railroads*—Chicago & Grand Trunk; Great Western of Canada—occupy same depot; Grand Trunk; Port Huron & Northwestern—occupy separate depots. *Business interests*—Commercial, shipbuilding, manufacturing, lumber, &c. Twelve miles to St. Clair Mineral Springs.

Hotels—**Huron, Albion, Pacific, Commercial.**

PORT JERVIS, N. Y. Situated on the Delaware River, and on the Delaware and Hudson Canal. Population, 8677.

Hotels—**Delaware, Fowler, Union.**

PORTLAND, Me. Situated on Casco Bay. A port of entry. Population, 33 810. *Railroads*—Eastern ; Maine Central ; Portland & Ogdensburg—occupy same depot ; Boston & Maine—occupies separate depot on same street, opposite ; Portland & Rochester—occupies separate depot ; Grand Trunk—has a separate local depot, but through cars connect without change. *Business interests* —Mercantile, commercial and manufacturing.

Hotels—**Falmouth, United States, City.**

PORTLAND, Oregon. Situated on the Willameto River, 12 miles above its mouth, and 642 miles from San Francisco. Population, 20,500. *Railroads*—Oregon & California ; Oregon Railway & Navigation Co.; Northern Pacific. *Business interests*—Manufacturing and mercantile. There is a fine view of the Cascade Mountains from the city, five snow-clad peaks being in sight.

Hotels—**Clarendon, Occidental, St. Charles, Holton, Esmond.**

PORTSMOUTH, N. H. Situated on the Piscataqua River, three miles from the Ocean. The only seaport town in the State. Population, 9732.

Hotels—**Rockingham, Kearsage, National.**

PORTSMOUTH, O. Situated on the Ohio River, at

For advertising space in this work address the National Directory Co., New York City.

the mouth of Scioto River, also on the Ohio and Erie Canal. Population, 11,314. *Railroads*—Marietta & Cincinnati; Scioto Valley—occupy separate depots. *Business interests*—Commercial, manufacturing and mercantile.

Hotels—**Central, Biggs House, Massie House.**

PORTSMOUTH, Va. Situated at the mouth of Elizabeth River, opposite Norfolk. Population, 11,388. *Railroad*—Seaboard & Roanoke. *Business interests*—Commercial. The United States Navy Yard is located at Gosport, a suburb of Portsmouth.

Hotels—**American, Peabody.**

POTTSTOWN, Pa. Situated on the Schuylkill River. Population, 7214.

Hotels—**Madison, Merchants', Farmers'.**

POTTSVILLE, Pa. Situated on the Schuylkill River, at the mouth of Norwegian Creek. Population, 13,253. *Railroad*—Philadelphia & Reading. *Business interests*—Manufacture of iron, mining and mercantile. It is noted for its beautiful situation and immense coal trade.

Hotels—**Exchange, Merchants', Penn's.**

POUGHKEEPSIE, N. Y. Situated on a fine plateau overlooking the Hudson, midway between New York and Albany. Population, 20,207. The manufactories, notably iron, glass and farming tools, are extensive, but Poughkeepsie is chiefly famous as an academic city. Besides the celebrated Vassar college, there are three other academies for women, a military institute and a national business college. *Daily Newspapers*—Eagle ; News (morning) ; Press (evening). The State Insane Asylum overlooks the Hudson two miles north of the city.

Hotels—**Nelson House, Poughkeepsie.**

This work is circulated gratuitously among prominent hotels of the United States.

PROVIDENCE, R. I. Semi-capital of State. Situated on both sides of the Providence River, at the head of Narragansett and Providence Bays, thirty-five miles from the Ocean. A port of entry. Population, 104,850. *Railroads*—Boston & Providence; New York & New England; Providence & Springfield; Providence & Worcester; New York, Providence & Boston—all occupy same depot; Providence, Warren & Bristol—occupies separate depot. *Business interests*—Commercial and manufacturing.

Hotels—**Narragansett, City, Dorrance, Aldrich, Providence.**

PUEBLO, Col. Situated on the Arkansas River. Population, 7821.

Hotels—**Lindell, Pittsburg,** in Pueblo proper; **Globe, Grand Central,** and **Victoria,** in South Pueblo.

QUEBEC, Que. Capital of Province of Quebec. Situated on the St. Lawrence River, at the mouth of the St. Charles River, 340 miles from the ocean. Population, 75,000. *Railroads*—Grand Trunk; Quebec, Montreal, Ottowa & Occidental,—occupy separate depots. *Business interests*—Mercantile, commercial, ship building, lumber, &c. The city has a remarkably picturesque situation between the two rivers, at the north-east extremity of a narrow but elevated table-land, which for about eight miles forms the left bank of the St. Lawrence.

Hotels—**Albion, Russell, St. Louis.**

QUINCY, Ill. Occupies a commanding situation upon the east bank of the Mississippi River, 170 miles above St. Louis. Population, 27,275. *Railroads*—Chicago, Burlington & Quincy; Hannibal & St. Joseph; St.

For advertising space in this work address the National Directory Co., New York City.

Louis, Keokuk & North-western; Wabash, St. Louis & Pacific,—all roads occupy same depot. *Business interests* —Manufacturing, commercial and agricultural.
Hotels—**Tremont, Windsor.**

QUINCY, Mass. Bordering on Quincy Bay in Boston Harbor, eight miles south-east of Boston. Population, 10,529. *Railroads*—Old Colony. *Business interests*— Manufacturing boots and shoes, granite quarries, &c.
Hotels—**Old Squantum, Wollaston, Robertson, New Squantum, Atlantic, Great Hill, Albion, Linden, Willow, Beach.**

RACINE, Wis. Situated on Lake Michigan, at the mouth of Root River. Population, 16,031. *Railroads*— Chicago, Milwaukee & St. Paul; Chicago & North-western—occupy separate depots. *Business interests*—Manufactures of various kinds. Racine is noted for manufacture of agricultural machines.
Hotels—**Blake, Huggin's House** ($2 per day); **Commercial** ($2 per day).

RAHWAY, N. J. Situated upon both sides of the Rahway River. Population, 6430.
Hotels—**Chamberlain's, Crowell's, Park House.**

RALEIGH, N. C. Capital of State. Situated a few miles from the Neuse River. Population, 12,000. *Railroads*—Raleigh & Augusta Air-Line; Raleigh & Gaston; Richmond & Danville—occupy same depot. *Business interests*—Mercantile and manufacturing (tobacco). The State Lunatic Asylum, Institution for the Deaf, Dumb and Blind and State Penitentiary are located here.
Hotels—**Central, Exchange, Yarboro.**

This work is circulated gratuitously among prominent hotels of the United States.

RANDOLPH, Mass. Population, 4022.
Hotel—**Howard**.

READING, Pa. Situated on the Schuylkill River and Canal. Population, 43,280. *Railroads*—Philadelphia & Reading; Wilmington & Northern—street car connection between depot. *Business interests*—Manufacturing, principally iron, wool, hats and woolen goods.

Hotels—**American** (Rates $2 per day); **Mansion, Keystone, Grand Central, Merchants'**.

RED WING, Minn. Situated on the Mississippi River. Population, 5811.
Hotels—**St. James** ($2 and $2.50 per day); **Hickman House**.

. RENO, Nev. Situated on the Truckee River. Population, 3000.
Hotels—**Arcade, Depot, Lake House**.

RICHFIELD SPRINGS, N. Y. A summer watering place 1600 feet above the sea. Population, 1500. There is here a noted sulphur spring.
Hotels—**New American, Central, National, Richfield, Spring, Davenport, Tuller, Johnson, Dutkirk**.

RICHMOND, Ind. Situated on the White Water River. Population, 12,743. *Railroads*—Cincinnati, Hamilton & Dayton; Grand Rapids & Indiana; Pittsburg, Cincinnati & St. Louis—occupy same depot. *Business interests*—Mercantile and manufacturing.
Hotels—**Bryson, Githens, Arlington, Grand, Huntington**.

RICHMOND, Va. Situated on the James River. Population, 63,803. *Railroads*—Richmond & Petersburg;

For advertising space in this work address the National Directory Co., New York City.

Richmond, Fredericksburg & Potomac,—occupy same depot; Chesapeake & Ohio; Richmond & Danville; Richmond, York River & Chesapeake—occupy separate depots; Richmond, Fredicksburg & Potomac and Richmond & Danville connect near Belle Island, opposite Richmond. *Business interests*—Mercantile and Manufacturing.

Hotels—**American, Ford's, Exchange and Ballard.**

ROCHELLE, Ill. Population, 1896.
Hotels—**Rocket, Rochelle.**

ROCHESTER, Minn. Situated on the Zumbro River. Population, 5198.
Hotels—**Park Place, Bradley, Cook, Peirce.**

ROCHESTER, N. H. Population, 4200.
Hotels—**Dodge's, Mansion, Wrisley.**

ROCHESTER, N. Y. Finely situated on both banks of the Genesee River at the Falls, seven miles from Lake Ontario. It has a population of 89,363, many fine buildings, costly churches and three convents. *Railroads*—New York, West Shore & Buffalo; New York Central; New York, Lake Erie & Western, (Corning branch); Rochester & Lake Ontario; Rochester & Pittsburg; Buffalo, New York & Philadelphia; Rome, Watertown & Ogdensburg; Genesee Valley, each having a separate station in the city. The Erie Canal crosses the Genesee River at Rochester by means of an aqueduct, constructed at great expense by the State. From Charlotte, the port of Rochester, at mouth of Genesee River, on Lake Ontario, a large shipping trade is carried on with Canada and the Upper Lakes. The manufactories are extensive and varied, but Rochester takes pre-eminence among cities of the world for its flour mills and its 1500 acres of nurseries which send away fruits, plants and young trees, to the value of $2,500,000 annually. The University of Rochester, and Rochester Theological Seminary, are flourishing institutions, taking rank with the foremost of their kind in the State; there are also twenty-nine public school buildings.

Hotels—**Powers, Lieders'** (Rates $2 to $3 per day); **Osburn House, Whitcomb, National, Congress Hall, Brackett, Waverly House.**

ROCHESTER, Pa. Situated between the Ohio and Beaver Rivers. Population, 2500.

Hotels—**Pavalion. St. James, Doncaster House.**

ROCKFORD, Ill. Situated on Rock River. Population, 13,136. *Railroads*—Chicago & North-western; Chicago & Iowa; Chicago, Milwaukee & St. Paul—latter two occupy same depot. *Business interests*—Manufacturing.

Hotels—**Holland, Edwards', American, Commercial, City.**

ROCK ISLAND, Ill. Situated on the Mississippi River, two miles above the mouth of the Rock River, at the foot of Rock Island and the upper rapids, opposite the city of Davenport. Population, 11,660. *Railroads*—Chicago, Rock Island, & Pacific; Chicago, Milwaukee & St. Paul (Racine & South western Div.),—occupy same depot. Rock Island & Mercer County, Rock Island & Peoria—occupy same depot; Chicago, Burlington & Quincy (St. Louis Line)—separate depot. *Business interests*—Manufacturing and mercantile.

Hotels—**Harper House, Commercial, Rock Island.**

For advertising space in this work address the National Directory Co., New York City.

ROCKLAND, Me. Situated on the Penobscot Bay. Population, 7650.
Hotels—**Lycde, Lindsay House, Thorndike House.**
ROME, Ga. Situated on the Coosa River. Population, 4374.
Hotels—**Rome, Central House.**
ROME, N. Y. Situated on the Mohawk River and Black River canal. The population of 12,045 has a somewhat cosmopolitan character. *Railroads*—The N. Y. Central & Rome, Watertown & Ogdensburg R. R. trains leave the same station, opposite the depot of Del., Lack, & Western R'y. *Business interests*—Large rolling mills, railroad shops, woolen knitting factories, and a prosperous country trade is carried on.
Hotels—**Commercial, Willette, Curtis, Stanwix Hall.**
ROSENDALE. N. Y. Situated on Rondout Creek and the Delaware and Hudson Canal. Population, 720.
Hotels—**Abe Lammon's, Conrad Shinnen's.**
RUTLAND, Vt. Situated on Otter Creek. Population, 12,000. *Railroads*—Central Vermont ; Bennington & Rutland—Delaware & Hudson Canal Co.—occupy same depot. *Business interests*—Quarrying marble and slate, manufacturing and mercantile.
Hotels—**Bardwell, Bates, Berwick.**
SACO, Me. Situated on the Saco River, opposite Biddeford. Population, 5757.
Hotel—**Saco House.**
SACRAMENTO, Cal. Situated on the Sacramento River, one mile below the confluence of the Sacramento and American Rivers. Population, 21,420. *Railroads*—

This work is circulated gratuitously among prominent hotels of the United States.

Central Pacific (and its branches—the California Pacific, Oregon Division, and Sacramento Valley); Sacramento & Placerville; Southern Pacific—Union depot. *Business interests*—Mercantile, manufacturing, and agricultural.

Hotels—**Capital, Golden Eagle, Union, Western, State, Pacific, The Langham.**

SAGINAW CITY, Mich. Situated on the Saginaw River, two miles above East Saginaw. Population, 10,525. *Railroads*—Detroit & Bay City; Flint and Pere Marquette; Michigan Central; Saginaw Valley and St. Louis—occupy same depot. *Business interests*—Lumber, salt, &c.

Hotels—**Crowley, Kirby, Taylor, American, Dunbar.**

ST. ALBAN'S, Vt. Situated three miles from Lake Champlain. Population, 7201.

Hotels—**American, Welden, St. Alban's, Central.**

ST. CATHERINES, Ont. Located on the Welland Canal. Population, 15,000. *Railroads*—Great Western of Canada; Welland—occupy separate depots. *Business interests*—Manufacturing, mercantile, agricultural and ship building.

Hotels—**Cairns, Murray, Spring Bank, Stephenson, Welland.**

ST. CHARLES, Mo. Situated on the Missouri River. Population, 7652.

Hotels—**Galt, St. Charles, Merchants', Monroe, Western, California House, Strangers' Home.**

ST. CLAIR, Mich. Situated on St. Clair River, 60

For advertising space in this work address the National Directory Co., New York City.

miles north-easterly from Detroit, and 12 miles south from Port Huron. Population, 3000.
Hotel—**The Oakland.**

ST. CLOUD, Minn. Situated on the west bank of the Mississippi River. Population, 2464.
Hotels—**Central, Minnesota, Schafer,**

ST. JOHN, N. B. Situated on the Bay of Fundy, at the mouth of the St. John River. Population, 28,805. *Railroads*—St. John & Maine, Intercolonial—occupy separate depots. *Business interests*—Lumber, ship-building, fishing and mining.
Hotels—**Dufferin, Park, Waverley House, New Victoria, Revere House, Royal Globe, International.**

ST. JOHNS, Quebec. Situated on the Richelieu River, the outlet of Lake Champlain. Population, 4100.
Hotels—**St. John, United States, American.**

ST. JOHNSBURY, Vt. Situated on the Passumpsic River. Population, 5806.
Hotels—**St. Johnsbury, Avenue, Cottage Hotel.**

ST. JOSEPH, Mo. Situated on the Missouri River. Population, 32,484. *Railroads*—Kansas City, St. Joseph & Council Bluffs; Union Pacific; Hannibal & St. Joseph; Missouri Pacific; Wabash, St. Louis & Pacific; St. Joseph and Des Moines—occupy Union depot. *Business interests*—Manufacturing, mercantile, agriculture, stock raising, pork packing, &c.
Hotels—**Pacific, World's, Bacon, Central, Saunder's, Occidental.**

ST. LOUIS, Mo. Situated on the west bank

This work is circulated gratuitously among prominent hotels of the United States.

of the Mississippi River, 20 miles below the entrance of the Missouri, and 174 miles above the mouth of the Ohio. A port of entry. Population, 350.522. *Railroads*—Chicago & Alton ; Chicago, Burlington & Quincy (St. Louis & Rock Island Division) ; Cairo & St. Louis ; Illinois & St. Louis ; Indianopolis & St. Louis ; Missouri Pacific ; Ohio & Mississippi ; St. Louis and San Francisco , St. Louis, Iron Mountain & Southern ; St. Louis and South-eastern ; St. Louis, Vandalia, Terre Haute; and Indianapolis, St. Louis, Alton & Terre Haute; Wabash, St. Louis & Pacific—all roads occupy Union Depot. *Business interests*—Manufacturing, mercantile, commercial, &c. By the Mississippi and Missouri Rivers, and their affluents, it is the converging point of nearly fifteen thousand miles of steamboat navigation. Its river craft plying between this and other points numbers 647 vessels, of which 209 are steamers, and 438 barges, all valued at $6,844,200, with a carrying capacity of 236,960 tons. According to the census returns of 1870, St. Louis had one thousand manufacturing firms, with an invested capital of $48,387,150.

Hotels—Southern, Lindell, Laclede, Planters, Barnum's, St. James.

ST. PAUL, Minn. Situated on the Mississippi River, 13 miles below the Falls of Saint Anthony. Population, 41,408 *Railroads*—Chicago, Milwaukee & St. Paul (Prairie du Chien and La Crosse Division), Chicago St. Paul, Minneapolis & Omaha Line ; St. Paul Minneapolis & Manitoba ; Northern Pacific, and St. Paul & Duluth occupy Union depot. All trains enter St. Paul on the

For advertising space in this work address the Na'ional Directory Co., New York City.

levee. *Business interests*—Wholesale trade, railroad, and manufactures.
Hotels—Metropolitan, Merchants' Grand Central, International, Clarendon, Windsor.

ST. STEPHEN'S, N. B. Situated on the St. Croix River. Population, 6000.
Hotels—Commercial, Queen.

ST. THOMAS, Ont. Population, 7200.
Hotels—Commercial, Queens, Hutchinson, Lisgar, Penwarden, Wilcox.

SALAMANCA, N. Y. Population, 2800.
Hotels—Dudley, Kreiger, Haymacker, Oil Exchange, Brookty.

SALEM, Mass. Situated chiefly on a strip of land formed by two inlets of the sea called North and South Rivers. A port of entry. Population, 27,598. *Railroads*—Boston & Lowell ; Eastern (Lawrence Branch), —occupy same depot ; Eastern (South Reading Branch), —occupies separate depot. *Business interests*—Manufacturing and mercantile.
Hotels—Essex, Derby, Salem, Farragut, Central.

SALEM, N. J. Situated on the Salem River two and a half miles from Delaware Bay. Population, 6649.
Hotels—Garwood's, Nelson, Schaeffer's.

SALEM, Ore. Situated on the Willamette River and Oregon & California R. R. This city has fine educational advantages. including the Willamette University, Women's College and Sisters' school. The State prison is also located here.
Hotels—Chemeketa, Reed.

This work is circulated gratuitously among prominent hotels of the United States.

SALISBURY, N. C. Population, 2777.
Hotels—**Boyden, National.**

SALT LAKE CITY, Utah. Situated on the Jordan River. Population, 20,768. *Railroads*—Utah Central; Utah Southern, Utah Western—occupy same depot. *Business interests*—Mercantile and manufacturing.
Hotels—**Walker, Continental, White, Warsatch, Clift, Overland, Valley.**

SAN ANTONIO, Tex. Situated on the San Antonio River, which has its source a few miles above the city. Population, 35,000. *Railroads*—Galveston, Harrisburg & San Antonio ; International & Great Northern—separate depots. *Business interests*—Mercantile. The U. S. Government has an arsenal located here, and it is the headquarters of the army in Texas. San Antonio is one of the oldest cities in the United States, and has much to interest the stranger. The chief interest centres in the Missions, five in number, built in the eighteenth century.
Hotels—**Hotel Maverick, Menger, Hord's, Central, Vance.**

SANDUSKY, O. Situated on Sandusky Bay of Lake Erie. Population, 15,838. *Railroads*—Baltimore & Ohio ; Cincinnati, Sandusky & Cleveland ; Lake Shore & Michigan Southern, and Lake Erie & Western—last two occupy same depot ; others separate. *Business interests*—Commercial, agricultural and manufacturing, including large iron and steel works.
Hotels—**Sloan House, Colton, West House.**

SAN FRANCISCO, Cal. Situated on San Francisco Bay. Population, 233,956. *Railroads*—Central Pacific ;

For advertising space in this work address the National Directory Co., New York City.

North Pacific Coast; San Francisco and North Pacific; South Pacific Coast; Southern Pacific—occupy separate depots. *Business interests*—Commercial, mercantile, manufacturing.

Hotels—**Grand Hotel, Palace, Lick, Baldwin, Occidental, Russ.**

SAN JOSE, Cal. Situated on the Guadalupe River, fifty miles south of San Francisco. Population, 12,567. *Railroads*—Central Pacific; Southern Pacific—occupy same depot; South Pacific Coast—occupies separate depot. *Business interests*—Mercantile and agricultural.

Hotel—**Pacific Hotel.**

SANTA ROSA, Cal.—Situated on Santa Rosa Creek. Population, 3474.

Hotels—**American, Grand, Occidental, Santa Rosa.**

SARATOGA SPRINGS, N. Y. Population, 10,822. *Railroads*—Adirondack; Delaware & Hudson Canal Co.; Boston, Hoosac Tunnel & Western; Saratoga, Mt. McGregor & Lake George.

Hotels—**American, Clarendon, United States, Congress Hall, Grand Union, Windsor, Adelphi, Arlington** ($3 per day), **Columbiana, Commercial** ($2.50 per day), &c.

SARNIA, Ont. Situated on the St. Clair River, opposite Port Huron, Mich. A port of entry. Population, 4500.

Hotels—**Alexander, Bell, Royal, Chapman.**

SAVANNAH, Ga. Situated on the Savannah River, eighteen miles above its mouth. A port of entry. Population, 30,081. *Railroads*—Savannah, Florida & West-

This work is circulated gratuitously among prominent hotels of the United States.

ern; Savannah & Charleston—occupy same depot; Central of Georgia—occupies separate depot. *Business interests*—Shipping of cotton, rice, lumber and naval stores.

Hotels—**Pulaski, Screven, Marshall, Harnett, Pavillion, European, Planters.**

SCHENECTADY, N. Y. Situated on the Mohawk River and the Erie Canal. Population, 13,675. The N. Y. Central R. R. (Main Line and Troy Branch) and the Del. & Hudson Canal Co. R. R. share same station; New York, West Shore & Buffalo; Delaware & Hudson Canal Co.—same depot. *Business interests*—Manufacturing woolen goods, iron foundries and railroad shops.

Hotels—**Givens', Carley.**

SCRANTON, Pa. Situated on the Lackawanna River. Population, 45,850. *Railroads*—Delaware and Hudson Canal Co.; Delaware, Lackawanna & Western—occupy same depot; Central of New Jersey—occupies separate depot. *Business interests*—Mining, manufacturing and mercantile.

Hotels—**Wyoming, Forest ($2 per day), St. Charles, Lackawanna Va'ley, Susquehanna, Scranton.**

SEDALIA, Mo. Population, 15,000. *Railroads*—Missouri Pacific; Kansas & Texas Div. of Mo. Pac.—occupy same depot; Sedalia, Warsaw & Southwestern Div. of Missouri Pacific—occupies separate depot. *Business interests*—Mercantile, agricultural and manufacturing.

Hotels—**Kaiser, Garison, Jay Gould, Lindell, Leroy, City.**

SELMA, Ala. Situated on the Alabama River. Population, 7500.

Hotels—**St. James ($2.50 per day), Southern.**

For advertising space in this work address the National Directory Co. New York City.

SENECA FALLS, N. Y. Situated on the Seneca River. Population, 5896.
Hotels—Globe, Hoag House.

SHARON, Pa. Situated on the Shenango River. Population, 5711.
Hotels—Messer House, Carver House, Shenango House.

SHAMOKIN, Pa. Situated on Shamokin Creek. Population, 9000.
Hotels—National, United States, City, Curtis, Anthracite, Gap.

SHEBOYGAN, Wis. Situated on Lake Michigan, at the mouth of the Sheboygan River. Population, 7326.
Hotels—Beekman, Park, Kossuth, Washington, Franklin, Wisconsin.

SHELBY, Mich. Situated on the Chicago & West Michigan R. R., half way between White Hall and Pentwater. Population, 800.
Hotels—The Elliot House, Moore's.

SHELBYVILLE, Ind. 27 miles south of Indianapolis, on Blue River. Population, 5000.
Hotel—Roy House.

SHELBYVILLE, Tenn. Situated on the Duck River. Population, 2836.
Hotels—Evans House, Barksdale House.

SHENANDOAH, Pa. Population, 10,148. *Railroads*—Lehigh Valley ; Philadelphia & Reading—occupy separate depots. *Business interests*—Mining (coal).
Hotels—Merchants', National, United States, Philadelphia, Shenandoah Valley, Central.

This work is circulated gratuitously among prominent h tels of the United States.

SHERBROOKE, Que. Situated on both sides of the River Magog and River St. Francis. Population, 7500.
Hotels—Continental, Passumpsic, Magog House, Sherbrooke House.

SHERMAN, Tex. Population, 7006.
Hotels—Beiler, Binkley, New Southern, Sherman.

SHREVEPORT, La. Situated on the Red River. Population, 11,017. *Railroads*—Texas & Pacific; New Orleans Pacific. *Business interests*—Commercial and mercantile. About 100,000 bales of cotton are shipped from this point annually, and immense numbers of Texas cattle are shipped.
Hotels—Cumpston's, Pacific.

SIDNEY, O. Situated on Miami River. Population, 5000.
Hotel—Burnett.

SIOUX CITY, Ia. Situated on the Missouri River. Population, 7381.
Hotels—Hubbard, Merchants, St. Elmo, Madison, Davenport, Chicago.

SIOUX FALLS, Dakota. Situated on the Big Sioux River, at the head of the Big Sioux Falls. Population, 5,500.
Hotels—Cataract ($2 and $2.50 per day), Sherman, Central, Merchants', Phillips.

SMYRNA, Del. Population, 2500.
Hotels—Delaware, Smyrna House.

SOUTH BEND, Ind. Situated on the St. Joseph River, at its southern bend, hence the name "South Bend." Population, 13,279. *Railroads*—Chicago & Grand

---

For advertising space in this work address the National Directory Co., New York City.

Trunk; Lake Shore & Michigan Southern; Michigan Central—occupy separate depots. *Business interests*—Manufacturing, mercantile and agricultural.

Hotels—**Grand Central, St. James, Oliver, Dwight.**

SOUTH NORWALK, Ct. Situated on the Norwalk River. Population, 5300.

Hotels—**City** ($2 per day), **Bartlett, Mahackemo** ($2 to $3 per day), **Warwick.**

SPARTA, Wis. Situated on the La Crosse River. Population, 2384.

Hotels—**Warner House, Ida House.**

SPOKANE FALLS, W. T. Situated on the Spokane River and on Idaho division of the Northern Pacific Railroad, 1537 miles west from St. Paul. The river at this place falls, within the space of half a mile, 150 feet, affording unlimited water power for manufacturing, which is carried on quite extensively.

Hotels—**Sprague House, California House, Western.**

SPRINGFIELD, Ill. Capital. Population, 19,746. *Railroads*—Chicago & Alton—occupies separate depot; Illinois Central; Ohio & Mississippi—occupy same depot; Springfield & Northwestern; Wabash; St. Louis & Pacific—occupy same depot. *Business interests*—Mercantile and manufacturing. A handsome monument in honor of President Lincoln is an object of especial interest. His remains are deposited beneath the monument.

Hotels—**Leland** ($2.50 and $3 per day), **Revere** ($2 ($2 per day), **St Nicholas.**

SPRINGFIELD, Mass. Situated on the Connecticut River. Population, 33,340. *Railroads*—Boston & Albany;

This work is circulated gratuitously among prominent hotels of the United States.

Connecticut River; New York, New Haven & Hartford—occupy same depot; New York & New England—occupies separate depot. *Business interests*—Manufacturing.

Hotels—**Massasoit, Warwick, Haynes, Cooley's.**

SPRINGFIELD, Mo. Population, 6000.

Hotels—**Lyon, Metropolitan, Southern, Transient, North Springfield.**

SPRINGFIELD, O. Situated on the Mad River, at the mouth of Lagonda Creek. Population, 20,729, *Railroads*—Indiana, Bloomington & Western; Cleveland, Columbus, Cincinnati & Indianapolis; Springfield Southern—occupy same depot; New York, Pennsylvania & Ohio; Pittsburg, Cincinnati & St. Louis—occupy same depot. *Business interests*—Manufacturing agricultural implements, turbine wheels, &c.

Hotels—**Lagonda, St. James.**

STAMFORD, Ct. Situated near the mouth of Mill River. Population, 11,298 *Railroads*—New York, New Haven & Hartford; New Canaan—occupy same depots. *Business interests*—Manufacturing and mercantile.

Hotels—**Stamford House** ($2 per day), **Union House** ($2 per day).

STAUNTON, Va. Population, 7767.

Hotels—**American, Virginia.**

STERLING, Ill. Situated near Rock River. Population, 5841.

Hotels—**The Galt, Wallace.**

STEUBENVILLE, O. Situated on the Ohio River, which is here about one thousand feet wide. Population, 12,017. *Railroads*—Cleveland & Pittsburg; Pitts-

For advertising space in this work address the National Directory Co., New York City.

burg, Cincinnati & St. Louis—occupy separate depots. *Business interests*—Manufacturing. The Pittsburg, Cincinnati & St. Louis Railroad shops are located here.

Hotels—**Cochran, Central, St. Nicholas, United States, Imperial, St. Charles.**

STILLWATER, Minn. Situated on the St. Croix River, at the head of Lake St. Croix. Population, 9059.

Hotels—**Pacific, Sawyer House.**

STOCKTON, Cal. Situated at the head of tide water in the San Joaquin Valley. Population, 10,287. *Railroads*—Central Pacific and its branches, the Stockton & Copperopolis and Stockton & Visalia—occupy separate depots. *Business interests*—Grain dealing and manufacture of agricultural implements, foundries and machinery &c. California State Insane Asylum and Nevada State Insane Asylum are located here.

Hotels—**Yosemite, Central, Commercial, Mansion House, Eagle.**

STONINGTON, Ct. Situated on Long Island Sound. A port of entry. Population, 1754.

Hotels—**Wadawannuck, Ocean.**

STOUGHTON, Mass. Population, 4869.

Hotels—**Drake's, Chemung, Stoughton.**

STRATFORD, Ont. Population, 9200.

Hotels—**Albion, Commercial, Mansion, Windsor, American, Avon, City, Royal, Exchange, Cabinet, Victoria.**

STREATOR, Ill. Situated on the Vermillion River. Population, 8000.

Hotels—**Streator, American, Central, Geiger, City.**

This work is circulated gratuitously among prominent hotels of the United States.

STROUDSBURG, Pa. Situated on Broadhead Creek. Population, 1860.
Hotels—Burnett, American, Washington, Indian Queen.

SUMTER, S. C. Population 2000.
Hotels—Sumter, Davis House, Jervey House.

SUNBURY, Pa. Situated on the Susquehanna River. Population, 4500.
Hotels—City, Central, Empire, Packer, Clement.

SYRACUSE, N. Y. Situated two miles from Onondaga Lake and at the junction of the Erie and Oswego canals. The city contains 51,791 inhabitants, nine banks, 42 churches and two convents. Location of the State Asylum for Idiots and the County Penitentiary. It is the seat of large and varied manufactures, extensive steel and iron works, and exports about 9,000,000 bushels of salt annually, this being the largest market in the United States. The New York Central and Rome, Watertown & Ogdensburg Railroads occupy contiguous stations; New York, West Shore & Buffalo—separate depot; the depot of the Del., Lackawanna & Western R'y (Syracuse, Binghamton & N. Y.) is one-quarter mile distant; the Syracuse, Chenango & N. Y. R. R. station half a mile from the others.
Hotels—Vanderbilt, Globe, Congress Hall, Empire.

TACOMA, W. T. Situated on Puget Sound, and is the junction of the Pacific and Cascade divisions of Northern Pacific Railroad. Tacoma is also the southern terminus of the Oregon Railway and Navigation Co.'s Steel steamers, running to Victoria, B. C., and end of line of Pacific Coast steamers between Puget Sound and San Francisco. *Business interests*—Mercantile and manfg.

For advertising space in this work address the National Directory Co., New York City.

Hotels—The Tacoma, Blackwell, Grand Central, Halstead House.

TALLAHASSEE, Fla. Population, 2750.
Hotel—City.

TAMAQUA, Pa. Population, 6019.
Hotels—United States, Beard's.

TAUNTON, Mass. Situated on the Taunton River, at the head of navigation. Population, 21,213. *Railroad*—Old Colony. *Business interests*—Manufacturing and commercial.
Hotels—City, St. Cloud, Central.

TERRE HAUTE, Ind. Situated on the Wabash River. Population, 26,040. *Railroads*—St. Louis, Vandalia, Terre Haute & Indianapolis; Indianapolis & St. Louis; Evansville, Terre Haute & St. Louis; Terre Haute & Southeastern; Illinois Midland. *Business interests*—Manufacturing; among the leading industries may be mentioned blast furnaces, rolling mills, nail factory, heading and stave mills, distillery, flouring mills, &c.
Hotels—Terre Haute, National ($2 per day), St. Clair.

TEXARKANA, Ark. Twelve miles from Red River. Population, 4000.
Hotels—Marquand, Draughon, Cosmopolitan, Benefield, Beidler.

THE DALLES, Ore. Situated on the Columbia River, at the junction of Mill Creek.
Hotels—Umatilla House, Cosmopolitan, Jackson, New Columbia.

THOMASVILLE, Ga. Population, 2325.
Hotels—Mitchell, Gulf.

This work is circulated gratuitously among prominent hotels of the United States.

THREE RIVERS, Mich. Population, 2525.
Hotel – Central House.

TIFFIN, O. Situated on the Sandusky River Population, 7875.
Hotels—Shawhan House, Empire House, Commercial.

TITUSVILLE, Pa. Situated on the both sides of Oil Creek, eighteen miles north of Oil City, and twenty-eight miles south of Corry on N. Y., P. & O. R. R. Population, 10,000. *Railroads*—Dunkirk, Allegheny Valley & Pittsburg; Buffalo, Pittsburg & Western—occupy separate depots. *Business interests*—Manufacturing and mercantile.

Hotels—European, Mansion, American.

TOLEDO, O. Situated on the Maumee River, six miles from Lake Erie. A port of entry. Population, 50,143. *Railroads*—Canada Southern (a division of the Michigan Central); Cincinnati, Hamilton & Dayton; Flint & Pere Marquette; Lake Shore & Michigan Southern; Wabash, St. Louis & Pacific—occupy same depot; Columbus, Hocking Valley & Toledo; Northwestern Ohio; Toledo and Ann Harbor—occupy same depot; Wheeling & Lake Erie; Michigan & Ohio—occupy same depot; Toledo, Cincinnati & St. Louis; Narrow Gauge— occupy separate depots; Ohio Central; Toledo & Indianapolis—occupy same depot at East Toledo. *Business interests*—The principal business interests are grain, the receipts of which are only below Chicago and Milwaukee; lumber, being the great market for Michigan pines and Wabash black walnut, the latter being shipped in unbroken cargoes to Europe. The manufacturing interests

---

For advertising space in this work address the National Directory Co., New York City.

are growing rapidly. The jobbing trade is very large. Shipbuilding and fishing interests are also extensive. The Maumee River furnishes at Toledo the finest harbor on the Great Lakes.

Hotels—**Merchant's, Boody House, Island House, Hotel Madison, Oliver House, Burnett House, American House.**

TOPEKA, Kan. Situated on the Kansas River. Population, 15,451. *Railroads*—Atchison, Topeka & Santa Fé; Kansas Pacific—occupy separate depots. *Business interests* — Manufacturing, iron-works, car-shops, etc. *Bank*—John D. Knox & Co. The Atchison, Topeka & Santa Fé Railroad shops are located here, also the College of the Sisters of Bethany. Topeka has the largest flouring mill interest in the State.

Hotels—**The Windsor, Fifth Avenue, Gordon, Copeland.**

TORONTO, Ontario. Situated on Lake Ontario. Population, 90,000. *Railroads*—Grand Trunk; Great Western of Canada; Northern of Canada; Toronto, Grey & Bruce; Toronto & Nipissing; Credit Valley—all roads occupy same depot. *Business interests*—Manufacturing, mercantile & Commercial.

Hotels—**Rossin, Queen's, American, Walker, Mansion.**

TOWANDO, Pa. Situated on the North Branch of the Susquehanna River. Population, 4000.

Hotels—**Elwell House, Ward House.**

TRENTON, N. J. Situated on the left bank of the Delaware River, thirty-three miles northeast of Philadelphia. Population, 29,910. *Railroads* — Pennsylvania;

This work is circulated gratuitously among prominent hotels of the United States.

Philadelphia & Reading. *Business interests*—Manufacturing, iron foundries and potteries. The Capitol building fronts State Street, and commands a fine view of the river.

Hotels—American House, National House, Tremont House, Trenton, United States, Clinton Street House, Revere House, State Street House.

TROY, N. Y. Situated on both sides of the Hudson River at the mouth of Poestenkill Creek, six miles above Albany, and at the head of steamboat navigation. Population, 56,747. *Railroads*—New York Central & Hudson River; Delaware & Hudson Canal Co.; Troy & Boston— occupy same depot. *Business interests*—Manufacturing, iron, and bessemer.steel, stoves, etc. The limits of the city extend about three miles along the river, and one mile from east to west.

Hotels — American, Mansion, Troy, Revere, Tremont, Union, International, Northern, Congress Hall, Exchange, Eagle.

TROY, O. Situated on the Miami River and Miami and Lake Erie Canal. Population, 4000.
Hotels—Hatfield, New Morris,

TRURO, N. S. Situated at the head of Cobequid Bay. Population, 5000.
Hotels—Grand Central, Intercolonial, Prince of Wales, Railway, Victoria, Parker House.

TYLER, Tex. Population, 2428.
Hotels—City, Ferguson's.

URBANA, O. Population, 6257.
Hotels—Exchange, Weaver.

For advertising space in this work address the National Directory Co., New York City.

UTICA, N. Y., on the Mohawk River and the Erie and Chenango canals. Population, 33,913. *Railroads*—New York Central & Hudson River; Utica & Black River—occupy same depot; Delaware, Lackawanna & Western; New York, West Shore & Buffalo—occupy separate depot. *Business interests*—Agricultural and manufacturing; latter consisting largely of shoe factories and woolen mills.

Hotels—Baggs, Butterfield, American.

VALPARAISO, Ind. Situated on Salt Creek. Population, 5500.

Hotels—Merchant's, Commercial, Fremont, Central.

VAN WERT, O. Population, 4875.

Hotels—De Puy, Van Wert, Adams, Hotel Avenue.

VICKSBURG, Miss. Situated on the Mississippi River. A port of entry. Population, 11,814. *Railroads*—Mississippi Valley & Ship Island; Vicksburg, Shreveport & Texas; Vicksburg & Meridian—occupy separate depots. *Business interests*—Shipping cotton, manufacturing cotton seed oil, mercantile, etc. The Mississippi Valley Yazoo River Packet Co. run eight steamers; the Memphis & St. Louis Packet Co., eight steamers; and the New Orleans & Vicksburg Packet Co., six steamers, all terminating their trips at this point.

Hotels—Lamadrid House, Pacific House, Washington Exchange.

VINCENNES, Ind. Situated on the Wabash River. Population, 7683.

Hotels—Grand, La Plante House, Junction House.

VIRGINIA CITY, Nev. Population, 13,705. *Railroad*

This work is circulated gratuitously among prominent hotels of the United States.

—Virginia & Truckee. *Business interests*—Silver mining and milling.
Hotels—American, Exchange, International,

WACO, Tex. Situated on the Brazos River. Population, 7317.
Hotels—McClelland, Central City, Taylor, Roper's European, Southern Pacific.

WAKEFIELD, Mass. Population, 5785.
Hotels—Leggett's, McMiller's.

WARREN, O. Situated on the Mahoning River. Population, 5000.
Hotels—Clifford House, National House, Austin House.

WARREN, Pa. Situated on the Allegheny River, at the mouth of Conewango Creek. Population, 4962.
Hotels—(four).

WARSAW, Ind. Population, 3119.
Hotels—Kirtley, Wright, Occidental.

WASHINGTON, D. C. Capital of United States. Situated on the Potomac River. Population, 147,307. Principal public buildings—Capitol, Presidents's Mansion, (White House), Treasury, War, Navy, Interior and Post Office Department, Patent Office, Smithsonian Institute, National Museum, &c. *Railroads*—Baltimore & Ohio,—separate depot; Baltimore & Potomac; Washington City, Virginia Midland & Great Southern—occupy same depot.
Hotels—Arlington, Ebbitt, Metropolitan, National, Willard's, Riggs, Imperial, St. James, Howard House, ($2.50 per day).

For advertising space in this work address the Na'ional Directory Co., New York City.

WASHINGTON, N. C. Situated on Pamlico River. Population, 2500.
Hotels—**River View, Adams.**

WASHINGTON, Pa. Situated on Chartiers Creek. Population, 4934.
Hotels—**Fulton, Valentine, Mansion.**

WATERBURY, Ct. Situated at the junction of Great Book, Mad and Naugatuck Rivers. Population, 20,269. *Railroads*—Naugatuck; New York & New England,—occupy separate depots. *Business interests*—Manufacturing brass, copper, clock, button, pin, and silver plated ware factories, &c.
Hotels—**Lawlor's, Myers', Earle House,** ($2 per day); **Scoville House,** ($2.50 to $3 per day); **Park,** ($1.50 per day); **Franklin House,** ($2 per day); **Smith's,** ($2 per day); **New England,** ($1 to $2 per day).

WATERLOO, Ia. Situated on both sides of the Cedar River. Population, 5631.
Hotels—**Central House, Logan House.**

WATERTOWN, N. Y. Situated on the Black River, near its entrance into Black River Bay. Population, 10,697. *Railroads*—Rome, Watertown & Ogdensburg; Utica & Black River,—occupy depots half a block apart. *Business interests*—Manufacturing and mercantile.
Hotels—**Globe, Harris, Kirby, Woodruff House, Crowner House.**

WATERTOWN, Wis. Situated on the Rock River. Population, 7868.
Hotels—**Commercial, Exchange, Watertown Junction House.**

This work is circulated gratuitously among prominent hotels of the United States.

WATKINS, N. Y. Situated at the head of Seneca Lake. Population, 2300. Seneca Lake Steam Navigation Co.'s steamers run from here to Geneva, over Seneca Lake. The famous summer resort, "Watkins Glen," is located here.

Hotels (Summer)—**Glen Mountain House**, (per day, $3 and $3.50), **Lake View, Glen Park**; (winter or all year round), **Fall Brook, Jefferson, Lake Shore.**

WAUKEGAN, Ill. Population, 4031.

Hotels—**Waukegan, Sherman, Lalle, German.**

WAUKESHA, Wis. Situated on the Fox River. Population, 3008. Noted as a resort for health and pleasure. The waters of the Waukesha are famous for their curative powers.

Hotels—**American, Mansion, National, Park, Fountain, Cambrian.**

WAVERLY, N. Y. Situated on the Chemung River, near its confluence with the Susquehanna River. Population, 4200.

Hotels—**American Commercial, Tioga, Warford.**

WEST CHESTER, Pa. Population, 7000. Remarkable for the beauty of its situation, the excellence of its schools, and the elegance of its public buildings.

Hotels—**Green Tree, Sherman, Turk's Head, Mansion, Eagle, West Chester.**

WESTFIELD, Mass. Population, 7641.

Hotels—**Central, Willmarth, Foster House.**

WESTMINSTER, Md. Situated at the source of the Patapsco River. Population, 2516. Western Maryland College is located here.

For advertising space in this work address the National Directory Co., New York City.

Hotels—**Central, Marsh's, Westminster City, Benford, Eastern, Anchor.**

WEST POINT, Ga. Situated on the Chattahoochee River. Population, 2200.

Hotels—**Chattahoochee House, Higginbotham House**

WEST POINT, N. Y. Situated on the Hudson River. It is picturesquely situated on commanding bluffs, and is noted as being the seat of the United States Military Academy, established in 1802; also, for the monuments and warlike relics which ornament its grounds, for the richness of its scenery and historic associations. A noted summer resort.

Hotels—**Cozzens, West Point.**

WHEELING, Capital of West Virginia. Is finely situated on the east bank of the Ohio River, at the mouth of Wheeling Creek. Population, 31,266. Wheeling is connected with Bellaire, Ohio, by a noble railroad bridge, which, including the approaches and a viaduct of forty-three arches, is one and three-quarter miles long. *Railroads*—Baltimore & Ohio, Pittsburg, Cincinnati & St. Louis, Cleveland & Pittsburg, (River Division), Wheeling & Lake Erie. *Business interests*—Extensive blast furnaces, iron foundries and forges, and manufactures of nails, glass-ware, steam engines, paper, leather, woolen goods, etc.

Hotels—**New McLure,** ($2, $2.50 and $3 per day). **St. James,** ($2 per day). **Stamm's.**

WHITE HALL, N. Y. Situated at the head of Lake Champlain, terminus of the Champlain Canal. Population, 4325.

Hotels—**Hall's Grand Opera, Grand Union, Yule's.**

This work is circulated gratuitously among prominent hotels of the United States.

WHITE MOUNTAINS, N. H. A group of isolated mountains a little north-east of the center of the State. The group proper extends only from fourteen to twenty miles, and from their sublimity and grandeur have received the cognomen of the "Switzerland of America." The altitudes of the several peaks in the group are Mt. Washington, 6226 feet, Mt. Jefferson, 5657 feet, Mt. Adams, 5759 feet, Mt. Madison, 5415 feet, Mt. Monroe, 5349 feet, Mt. Franklin, 4850 feet, Mt. Pleasant, 4712 feet.

Hotels—**Crawford, Fabyan, Twin Mountain Houses.**

WICHITA, Kan. Situated on the Arkansas River, at the mouth of the Little Arknansas River. Population, 6254.

Hotels—**Douglas Avenue, Occidental, Tremont.**

WICKFORD, R. I. Situated on an arm of Narragansett Bay, ten miles from the ocean. Population, 5000.

Hotels—**Mechanics', Washington.**

WILKES-BARRE, Pa. Situated on the North Branch of the Susquehanna River, opposite Kingston, Pa. Population, 23,339. *Railroads*—Central of New Jersey; Lehigh Valley, Penn.—have separate depots. *Business interests*—Manufacturing and coal mining.

Hotels—**Wyoming Valley, Luzerne, Exchange, Bristol.**

WILLIAMSPORT, Pa. Situated on the West Branch of the Susquehanna River, and on the West Branch Canal. Population, 18,934. *Railroads*—Northern Central; Pennsylvania (Philadelphia & Erie Div.)—occupy same

For advertising space in this work address the National Directory Co., New York City.

depot; Philadelphia & Reading—occupies separate depot. *Business interests*—Lumber and manufacturing.
Hotels—**Park, City** ($2 per day), **Crawford, Hepburn.**

WILLIMANTIC, Ct. Situated on the Willimantic River. Population, 5181.
Hotels—**Brainerd, Commercial, European, Sanderson.**

WILMINGTON, N. C. Situated on the Cape Fear River. A port of entry. Population, 17,361. *Railroads*—Carolina Central—occupies separate depot; Wilmington, Columbia & Augusta; Wilmington & Weldon—occupy same depot. *Business interests*—Naval stores and cotton, rice, peanuts and lumber.
Hotels-**Commercial, Purcell.**

WILMINGTON, Del. Situated on the Delaware River and Christiana and Brandywine Creeks, tributaries of the Delaware. Population, 42,499. *Railroads*—Delaware Western has separate depot; Wilmington & Northern; Philadelphia, Wilmington & Baltimore, Delaware Division of Penn. R. R. occupy same depot. *Business interests*—Iron ship building, car building, &c.
Hotels **Clayton, Delaware, European, United States.**

WINCHENDON, Mass. Situated on Miller's River. Population, 3200.
Hotels—**American, Tremont.**

WINCHESTER, Tenn. Situated on a branch on the Elk River. Population, 1378.
Hotels- **Webber, Ballard.**

This work is circulated gratuitously among prominent hotels of the United States.

WINCHESTER, Va. Population, 4949.
Hotels—Taylor, Hart, Grim's.

WINDSOR, Ont. Situated on the Detroit River, opposite Detroit, Mich. Population, 7000.
Hotels—**American, Great Western, International, Essex House.**

WINONA, Minn. Situated on the Mississippi River. Population, 10,208. *Railroads* — Chicago & Northwestern; Green Bay and Minnesota—occupy same depot; Chicago, Milwaukee & St. Paul—occupies separate depot. *Business interests*—Manufacturing, mercantile and agricultural.
Hotels—**Huff House, Jewell House.**

WINSTED, Ct. Situated at the outlet of Long Lake. Population, 4500, includes West Winsted.
Hotels—**Beardsley, Clarke, Winsted.**

WOBURN, Mass. Population, 10,938. *Railroad*—Boston & Lowell. *Business interests*—Manufacturing.
Hotel—**Central House.**

WOODSTOCK, Ont. Population, 6000.
Hotels—**Bishop's, Commercial, Royal, Carster House.**

WOONSOCKET, R. I. Situated on the Blackstone River. Population, 16,053. *Railroads*—Hopkinton, Milford & Woonsocket, New York & New England—occupy same depot; Providence & Worcester—occupies separate depot. *Business interests*—Manufacturing.
Hotels—**Monument, Woonsocket.**

WOOSTER, O. Population, 5933.
Hotels—**Archer, American, Central, Eastern.**

For advertising space in this work address the National Directory Co., New York City.

WORCESTER, Mass. Population, 58,295. *Railroads* —Boston & Albany; Boston, Barre & Gardner, and Monadnock; New York & New England; Providence & Worcester; Worcester & Nashua—occupy same depot; Worcester and Shrewsbury—occupies separate depot. *Business interests* Manufacturing.
Hotels—**Bay State, United States, Lincoln, Waldo, Waverly.**

XENIA, O. Population, 7026.
Hotels—**St. George, Commercial, Ohmer's.**

YANKTON, Dak. Situated on the Missouri River. Population, 4750.
Hotels—**Jencks', St. Charles, Merchants', Smithsonian.**

YONKERS, N. Y. Situated on the Hudson River, 15 miles above New York City. The population (18,892) is largely composed of New York City merchants and their families, whose villas line the picturesque heights above the river. *Railroads*—New York Central & Hudson River; New York City and Northern—occupy separate depots. *Business interests*—Manufacturing, principally hats, plows and silk. The old manor house in which Mary Philipse, the beautiful heiress of the estate, the heroine of Cooper's novel, "The Spy," and the early friend of George Washington, lived, is still much visited.
Hotels—**Gitty, Peabody, Mansion.**

YORK, Pa. Population, 13,940. *Railroads*—Northern Central; Pennsylvania (Northern Central Division)— occupy same depot; Peachbottom—separate depot.

This work is circulated gratuitously among prominent hotels of the United States.

Business interests—Manufacturing, mercantile and agricultural.
Hotels—**National, Metzell, Pennsylvania, Central, Washington.**

YOUNGSTOWN, O. Situated on the Mahoning River. Population, 15,431. *Railroads*—Ashtabula & Youngstown; Pitts., Fort Wayne & Chicago—occupies same depot; New York, Pennsylvania & Ohio; Pittsburg and Lake Erie—occupy same depot. Lake Shore & Michigan Southern; Painesville & Youngstown; Pitts., Cleve. & Toledo—occupy separate depots. *Business interests*—Coal mining and manufacturing railroad, pig, bar, band and hoop iron, brass, mowers and reapers, carriages, &c.
Hotels.—**Tod, Morton, Astor.**

YPSILANTI, Mich. Situated on the Huron River. Population, 5003.
Hotels—**New Hawkins, European, Barton.**

ZANESVILLE, O. Situated on the Muskingum River, and connected with Cleveland and the lakes by the Ohio Canal. Population, 18,120. *Railroads*—Baltimore and Ohio; Pittsburgh, Cincinnati & St. Louis—occupy separate depots. *Business interests*—Manufacturing iron, flour, machinery, agricultural implements, cotton and woolen fabrics, fruit canning, pork packing, &c.
Hotels **Clarendon, New Zane, American, Kirk.**

For advertising space in this work address the National Directory Co., New York City.

INDEX

— TO —

Advertising Directory and Buyer's Guide.

	PAGE.
Automatic Bank Punch Co.	37
Avery Machine Co. (Sewing Machines)	51
Brinkley, J., & Co. (Wagons, etc., etc.)	9
Blackman Disinfectant Co. of the United States	15
Bassett, Geo. F., & Co. (Crockery)	16
Blume & Co. (Cocoa)	42
Boston Cereal Mfg. Co. (Brown Bread Mixture)	47
Bastine & Co. (Flavoring Extracts)	48
Civiale Remedial Agency	17
Crane, M. (Stereotyping)	17
Dellac (Photographer)	7
Durham, Joseph T., & Co. (Tags, etc.)	12
Duparquet, L. F., & Huot (Cooking Ranges)	13
Dick & Fitzgerald (Publishers)	21
Dickinson, Geo. K. (Medicines)	43
Ehrets, Geo. (Brewery)	9
Eastwood, Benjamin (Laundry Machinery)	19
Fidelity and Casualty Co. (Insurance)	6
Fuchs, Frederick D. (Commission Merchant)	53
Grand Central Iron Works	8
Globe Novelty Co. ("Try Me" Burglar Alarm)	27

INDEX.

	PAGE.
Hartford Cold Spring Co. (Mineral Waters, etc.)	1
Holmes, F. P. (Inlaid Floors)	11
Hooper, Thomas (Picture Frames)	41
Hartfield, C. (Insect Powder)	41
Ham, John C. (Carriages)	52
Horton's Ice Cream	56
Imhauser, E. (Time Detector)	55
Johnson, Jacob K. (Monuments, etc.)	4
Jopson, Geo. W. (Key Rings)	53
Leathers, C. C. (Flour, etc.)	18
Libby, Dr. & Mrs. G. M. (Manicures)	30
Leach, J. (Stationer)	39
Lowey, Frederick (Electric Lights)	46
Luttgen, Fred'k Wm. (Champagnes)	54
Monumental Bronze Co.	20
Morehouse, Henry S. (Cabinets)	23
Mayer, D. A. (Wines)	45
Murtaugh, James, & Co. (Dumb Waiters)	56
Morison & Co. (Laundry Soap Powder)	49
Merriam, A., & Co. (Piano Stools, etc.)	52
New York Dyeing and Printing Establishment	8
Newman, A. (Watchman Time-keeper)	28, 29
New York Stencil Works	31
New York Conservatory of Music	44
O'Neil & Sullivan (Bookbinders)	5
Parker Bros. (Guns)	26
Pray, Dr. J. Parker (Manicure Goods)	34, 35
Peppers, C. H. (Linoleum)	3

INDEX.

	PAGE.
Phelps & Bartholomew (Water-meter Movements)	-14
Pease, Chas. G. (Fruits)	21
Prichard, J. H. (Steamer Chairs)	22
Planten (Empty Capsules)	24
Rigney & Wolff (Analytical Chemists)	56
Rockwood, Geo. G. (Photographer)	25
Smith, James (Chiropodist)	7
Stamford Foundry Co. (Stoves)	33
Shipman's Asa L., Sons (Fountain Pens)	38
Shriver & Co. (Copying Presses)	40
Stiles Galvanic Oil	43
Shaw, L. (Face Powder)	49
Thurston's Tooth Powder	24
The Smith & Egg Mfg. Co. (Locks, etc.)	32
The Judd Mfg. Co. (Athletic Goods)	36
United States Encaustic Tile Co	2
Walters, R. M. (Pianos, etc.)	10
Watkins, James Y., & Son (Hotel Kitchen Ware)	50
Zittel, Mme. B. (Manicure)	

H. M. WHEELOCK, Treas.   *J. B. WATSON, Man'gr.*

Hartford ❊ Cold ❊ Spring ❊ Co.

MANUFACTURERS OF

Ginger Ale, Sarsaparilla,

◄Lemon Soda and Table Waters►

MADE FROM

ABSOLUTELY PURE SPRING WATER,

Equal to all Foreign, and superior to all Domestic manufactures.

H. M. WHEELOCK & CO., Agts,

146 Chambers Street, N. Y.

Spring at HARTFORD, MAINE.

THE
United States Encaustic Tile Co.

MANUFACTURERS OF

Plain, Encaustic, Glazed, Enameled and Majolica

TILES

For Floors, Walls, Mantel Facings, Hearths, Stoves, &c.
and for Exterior Decoration.

Dealers, Architects and Contractors are respectfully invited to call and examine our stock, or address

W. W. LYON, - - - EASTERN MANAGER.

Office and Salesroom in

"THE CHELSEA," 228 WEST 23d STREET,

NEW YORK.

Manufactory, Indianapolis, Ind. Designs and Estimates Furnished.

C. H. PEPPER'S

LINOLEUM

— IS THE —

Cheapest & Best Floor Covering

IN THE WORLD.

1319 & 1321 Broadway, New York.

——AND——

72 Federal St., Boston, Mass.

THOMPSON'S ADVERTISING DIRECTORY

TELEPHONE CALL SPRING 108.

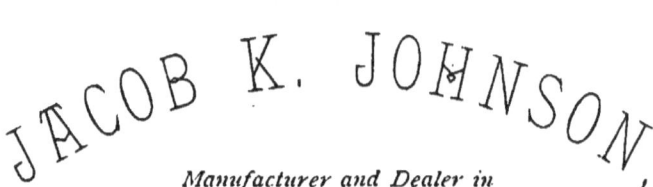

Manufacturer and Dealer in

Head and Tombstones,

LOTS ENCLOSED.

MARBLE AND GRANITE.

◄OFFICE AND WAREROOMS►

No. 396 BROOME STREET,

Near Centre   NEW YORK.

Jobbing promptly attended to, and work done at all Cemeteries.

JAMES O'NEIL. MICHAEL SULLIVAN.

O'NEIL & SULLIVAN,

BOOK ✢ BINDERS,

59 Beekman Street,

Cloth ✢ and ✢ School ✢ Work ✢ a ✢ Specialty.

GOODS RECEIVED AT 89 ANN STREET.

Fidelity & Casualty Company,
214 & 216 BROADWAY, NEW YORK.

W. M. RICHARDS, *Pres.*   J. M. CRANE, *Sec.*   R. J. HILLAS, *Ass. Sec.*

Cash Capital, $250,000.00, invested in U. S. Govern't Bonds.

$200,000 deposited with the N. Y. Ins. Department, for the Protection of Policy-holders.

Assets, January 1st, 1885,   -   - $512,026.11

FIDELITY GUARANTEE.

Bonds issued on the Fidelity and integrity of persons holding positions of public or private trust.
The Bonds of this Company are accepted by the Courts of the State of New York.
The rates of this Company are based on its own tested experience, as well as that of the leading British offices now existing.

ACCIDENT INSURANCE.

Giving indemnity for fatal or disabling injuries to persons.

DIRECTORS.

GEORGE T. HOPE,	Pres. Continental Ins. Co.
G. G. WILLIAMS,	Pres. Chemical Nat. Bank.
J. S. STRANAHAN,	Pres. Atlantic Dock Co.
A. B. HULL,	Retired Merchant.
DAVID DOWS,	Of David Dows & Co.
A. S. BARNES,	Of A. S. Barnes & Co.
H. A. HURLBUT,	Pres. of Com. of Emigration.
J. D. VERMILYE,	Pres. Merchants' Nat. Bank.
CHAS. DENNIS,	Vice-Pres. Atlantic Mut. Ins. Co.
ALEX. MITCHELL,	Pres. Chi., M. & St. P. R. R.
S. B. CHITTENDEN,	Ex.-M. C.
GEO. S. COE,	Pres. Am. Ex. Nat. Bank.
W. G. LOW,	Of Moore, Low & Sanford.
WM. M. RICHARDS,	President.

Actuary: *Fidelity Dep't:*   *Attorney:*
CAPEL E. Le JEUNE. W. HARVEY LEE, Sup't. JAMES A. BRADY.

Counsel: **MOORE, LOW & SANFORD.**

DELLAC,

Late Operator with ROCKWOOD.

Lightning Photographer

CHILDRENS PORTRAITS A SPECIAL STUDY.

No. 54 West 14th Street,

Three doors from Macy's,
Elevator from ground Floor,   *NEW YORK.*

JAMES SMITH,

Surgeon Chiropodist,

Office, No. 6 Cornelia Street, New York.

Cures Corns, Bunions, Ingrowing Nails and all diseases of the Feet.

By sending a postal card with address, parties will be attended to at their homes, without extra charge.

GRAND CENTRAL IRON WORKS,
JOSEPH MARREN,
157 East 44th Street,
ONE DOOR WEST OF 3D AVENUE,   NEW YORK.

COLUMNS, LINTELS, SILLS,

And all kinds of Work for Building, or other purposes, Stairs, Balconies, Shutters, Doors, Bank Vaults, &c. Plain and Ornamental Fire Escapes.

Also Manufacturers THE ADAMS PATENT CORRUGATED IRON FENCE and TREE GUARDS.

JOHN S. CLARK, Sec'y.   *JAMES T. YOUNG, Pres't.*

New York Dyeing & Printing Establishment
STATEN ISLAND.
No. 98 Duane St., New York.

BRANCH OFFICES:
- 870 late 752 Broadway, New York.
- 610 Sixth Avenue, New York.
- 168 Pierrepent Street, Brooklyn.
- 40 North Eighth St., Philadelphia.
- 7 Temple Place, Boston.
- 42 E Madison Street, Chicago.

Silk, Cotton & Woolen Dyeing in every variety executed promptly

MANUFACTURERS OF

BOOKBINDERS CLOTH,

IN ALL COLORS AND PATTERNS.

—⋅⋅THE⋅⋅—
BRINKLEY WAGON,
LATEST STYLE. BEST IMPROVEMENTS,
For $250.

Very stylish, and especially designed for gentlemen desiring a reliable, first-class road wagon at a low price. The many "Brinkley's" seen on the road in N. Y. City and elsewhere owned by the best known and most critical driving gentlemen prove their superior excellence. Every Wagon is warranted.

J. BRINKLEY & CO., 1593 Broadway, N. Y.

R. M. WALTERS,
◁PIANOS▷

57 and 59 University Place,

Cor. E. 12th Street,   NEW YORK.

PIANOS SOLD OR RENTED—CASH OR CREDIT.

A TRIBUTE TO THE NARVESEN PIANO.

MR. R. M. WALTERS, manufacturer of the Narvesen Pianos, at 57 and 59 University place, New York, has received a well-deserved compliment in the action of the Board of Education of this city, who have selected the Narvesen for the new Pianos required in our public schools. The pupils and schools as well as Mr. Walters should be congratulated on the choice made.

—*N. Y. Home Journal*, July 30th, 1884

F. P. HOLMES,

MANUFACTURER OF

Parquet or Inlaid Floors,

SOLID OR VENEERED IN THE EUROPEAN STYLE.

Wood Carpeting and Borderings for Rugs.

LAPE'S PAT'D FOLDING EXTENSIBLE LADDER.

OFFICES and STORES FITTED UP.

7 West 14th Street,

D. W. HOLMES,
Superintendent.

New York.

——— *ESTIMATES FREE.* ———

Shippers! Attention!!

$20 SAVED BY INVESTING $10
BY USING

Dunham's Patent Combination Tag & Envelope

Saves Postage, Envelopes, Addressing Letters, Sticking Stamps, Delivery to Postoffice.

Delivers Bill with Goods via Express one to three hours earlier than by Mail.

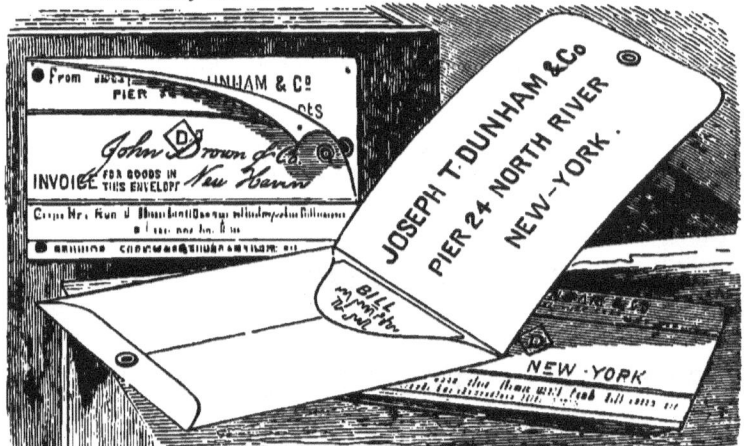

1,000,000 now in use in every part of the United States and Canada, in every line of trade. Duplicate orders now coming from first buyers in tenfold quantity.

Used in same manner as old style Denison Tag. Tie, Hook or Nail on Packages.

Now being used by first-class houses and found a perfect economiser.

Price, $10 per Thousand.

BUY OF OUR AGENTS OR SEND ORDERS TO

JOSEPH T. DUNHAM & CO.
SOLE MANUFACTURERS,
12 COURTLAND ST., - - NEW YORK.

Notice is hereby given that all infringements will be prosecuted to the full extent of the law.

L. F. DUPARQUET & HUOT,

MANUFACTURERS OF

FRENCH

Cooking Ranges

— AND —

BROILERS,

For Hotels, Steamboats, Families and Restaurants.

Also, COPPER, TIN and CAST IRON UTENSILS.

43 & 45 Wooster Street,

NEW YORK.

TURN THIS PAGE AROUND AND READ.

TURN THIS PAGE AROUND AND READ.

AND BUYERS GUIDE.   xv

THE
PASTEUR
RED CROSS
DISINFECTANT!

Combining BI-CHLORIDE OF MERCURY with other Chlorides so it can be used effectively; the only positive Disinfectant that meets the wants of the PUBLIC, and when used with the **BLACKMAN MACHINE**, WHICH WORKS AUTOMATICALLY, thoroughly cleanes Urinals or Closets every time it is used; and when used in our PATENT ATOMIZER just the thing for sick rooms, and a positive preventive of the spread of contagious diseases.

Send for Circular.

BLACKMAN DISINFECTANT CO., of U. S.,

Temple Court, 5 & 7 Beekman St.,

NEW YORK.

Geo. F. Bassett & Co.,

49 BARCLAY ST. and 52 & 54 PARK PLACE,

NEW YORK CITY.

—— IMPORTERS, EXPORTERS AND WHOLESALE DEALERS IN ——

China, Crockery and Glassware,

PLATED WARE, TABLE CUTLERY, &c.

For Hotels, Steamers and Restaurants.

WM. H. CROSS, MANAGER HOTEL DEPARTMENT.

IMPOTENT MEN

Be they Young or Old, having Lost those attributes of

PERFECT Manhood

MAY REGAIN QUICKLY

PERFECT

SEXUAL POWER !!!

AND

Procreative Ability,

Prof. Jean Civiale. BY THE USE OF

THE CIVIALE REMEDIES.

They cure every trace of **DEBILITY, SPERMATOR-RHŒA, VARICOCELE** and every form of Seminal loss and weakness whether due to Youthful Folly, Abuse, or Natural Failure. This treatment originated by **PROF. CIVIALE,** adopted in every **HOSPITAL** in **FRANCE** and unqualifiedly endorsed by the Medical Profession, is **EASILY APPLIED, PAINLESS, QUICK** and above all **LASTING IN ITS RESULTS.**

☞ **FREE TO ALL.** Upon receipt of 6 cents in postage stamps, we will send free to any earnest inquirer our splendid illustrated 64 page medical work, giving symptoms of all forms of Sexual Disease, description of this treatment, prices, testimonials and newspaper endorsements, &c., &c.

We are also agents for the new and certain to cure, Self-Adjusting and Glove Fitting Cradle Compressor, for the thorough and radical cure, without surgery, of

VARICOCELE

Consultation with full **MEDICAL STAFF, FREE.**
CIVIALE REMEDIAL AGENCY, 160 Fulton St., N. Y.

ELECTROTYPING and STEREOTYPING.

M. CRANE,

53, 55 and 57 Park Place, N. Y

ENTRANCE 21. COLLEGE PLACE.

Electrotyping and Stereotyping in all Branches.

THIS SPACE IS RESERVED FOR

C. C. LEATHERS,
No. 197 CHAMBERS STREET, NEW YORK,
Dealer in Flour, Pearl Meal Grits, &c.

AND BUYERS GUIDE. xix

BENJAMIN EASTWOOD,

METALLIC

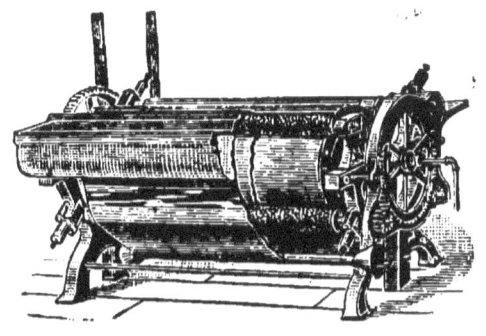

Laundry Machinery,

For HOTELS, Etc.

Silk Machinery, Shafting Pulleys, &c.

40 CORTLAND STREET,

New York.

—— SEND FOR CIRCULAR. ——

BOOKS.

The American Hoyle.—The only Standard authority on Games as played in America. By trumps   PRICE, $2.00

The Complete Poker Player.—A thorough and practical Treatise on the National Game. By JOHN BLACKBRIDGE.
PRICE, $1.00

Books will be mailed free to any address on receipt of the price by the Publishers,

DICK & FITZGERALD,
18 Ann Street, New York.

*** Send for complete illustrated Catalogue, mailed free.

CHAS. G. PEASE,
"The Fruiterer."
FOREIGN & DOMESTIC FRUITS, NUTS, FANCY GROCERIES, Etc.

☞ Orders executed promptly. Boxes packed for shipment to any part of the United States. Receiver of Direct Consignments of

FLORIDA ORANGES,
1300 Third Av. and 326 Greenwich St., NEW YORK.

Recommends BROOKVILLE SANATARIUM—Cancer a Specialty,
BROOKVILLE, IND.

⊲New York Agency⊳

OF THE

U. S. STEAMER CHAIR CO.

J. H. PRICHARD, 84 Broadway, N. Y.

Chairs marked and delivered on board of any Steamer at $2.50 each.

ORDERS BY MAIL PROMPTLY ATTENDED TO.

HARD WOOD VENEERED

Doors, Mantles and Cabinets,

FACTORY:

STATE STREET

MERIDEN, CONN.

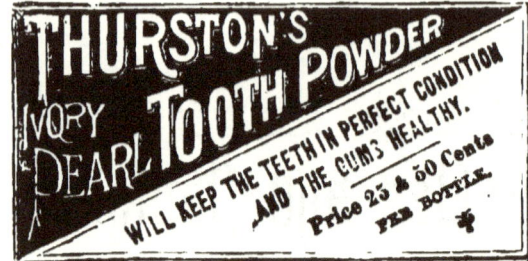

Sold by all

DRUGGISTS

AND

Fancy Stores.

This is a most excellent article for Cleansing and Preserving the Teeth. It hardens the gums, sweetens the breath, and beautifies the teeth. It contains no acid or harsh gritty substance — nothing that can injure the enamel in the slightest degree. By its constant use the teeth retain their efficiency and beauty, even to the extreme duration of life. It is put up in bottles, which prevents its being spoiled by exposure to the atmosphere, preserving its original combination of arts and its delicious flavor.

R. M. HOBBS'S MËEN FUN.

THE CELEBRATED
CHINESE
Skin & Toilet Powder
—FOR—
Preserving, Restoring and Beautifying the Complexion.

Boxes 25 Cents.   Sold by all Druggists and Fancy Goods Houses.

 **PLANTEN'S CAPSULES,**
Known as reliable since 50 years.

PLANTEN'S EMPTY CAPSULES

For taking medicine free of taste, smell, injury to the Teeth, Mouth or Throat. Send for Trial Box. Insist on PLANTEN's make.   100 by mail, 50 cents.

BLAIR'S PILLS,

Great English Remedy for Gout, Rheumatism and Kidney Complaints. Sure, prompt and effective.
Oval Boxes, 34 Pills, $1; Round Boxes, 14 Pills, 50c.
At all Druggists, and

PLANTEN'S, 224 William Street, New York.

ROCKWOOD

INSTANTANEOUS
CABINET PORTRAITS

REDUCED TO **$5** PER DOZEN.

☞ Mr. ROCKWOOD gives personal attention to the posing of sitters.

17 Union Square, N. Y.

Rockwood's Views of New York & Vicinity.

Over 600 Instantaneous Views of New York City—Public Buildings, Upper and Lower Harbor, Hudson River, &c., at 15 cts. to 50 cts. each.

Send for Catalogue.

GEO. G. ROCKWOOD,
Established 1859.   *17 Union Square.*

xxvi　THOMPSON'S ADVERTISING DIRECTORY

THE PARKER GUN.

At the Second International Clay Pigeon Tournament, held at New Orleans, La., Feb. 11th to 16th, 1885, the First Prize and Diamond Badge in the International Individual Championship, open to all the world, was won by B. Tiepel, with a Parker Gun. Among the contestants shooting other guns were such champions as Carver, Bogardus, Cody, Stubs, Erb, and others. During the entire tournament more prizes were won with Parker Guns, in proportion to the number used, than with any other gun.

PARKER BROS, Makers, · · Meriden, Conn.

NEW YORK SALESROOM, 97 CHANBERS STREET.

AND BUYERS GUIDE.   xxvii

Globe Novelty Co.
DEALERS IN

NOVELTIES
SPECIALTIES

Sole Agents for the

"Try Me"

AUTOMATIC

Burglar

Alarm.

FOR THE

Hardware

AND

Fancy Goods

TRADES.

Price, $1.50.

☞ Liberal discount to Agents and the Trade. Good reliable Agents wanted in every county.

OFFICE AND SALESROOM :

320 & 322 BROADWAY,
P. O. Box 2123.   *NEW YORK CITY.*

THE NEWMAN
Watchman Clock & Time Keeper

PATENTED MAY 18, 1880,

Is a handsome CLOCK, ten by ten inches, with a large plain Face or Dial, keeping good time ; has a double case to keep out Dust and Moisture, and is suitable for Office, Bank or Factory.

It is an *Indicator* which records the hours your Day or Night *Watchman* remains on duty, and is absolutely tamper-proof. Useful in Factories, Banks, Hotels, Theatres, Public Buildings, and all Institutions employing Watchmen.

Price, $10 Each.

Send for Circular. Address,

A. NEWMAN,
Box 130, - WILLIAMSBURGH, - New York.

The Newman Watchman Clock and Time Keeper,

85 SOUTH SIXTH STREET, BROOKLYN, E. D.

Manicures and Chiropodists,

1162 BROADWAY, - - NEW YORK.
377 BROADWAY, - - SARATOGA.

N. B.—Saratoga Office open from June 15th to September 15th

Mrs. Libby manufactures the following Preparations:

Mrs. Libby's Orient Pearl Powder, - 30c. per box
Mrs. Libby's Mendeline, - - - 50c. "
Mrs Libby's Cosmetic Opoline, - 50c. "
Mrs. Libby's Viola, - - - - 25c. per bot.
Mrs. Libby's Bristol Board, - - 25c. per box

CIRCULARS GIVING FULL PARTICULARS SENT FREE BY
— — ADDRESSING — —

Dr. & Mrs. G. M. Libby,
1162 BROADWAY, NEW YORK.

ADAMANTINE
Wheel Dating Stamp

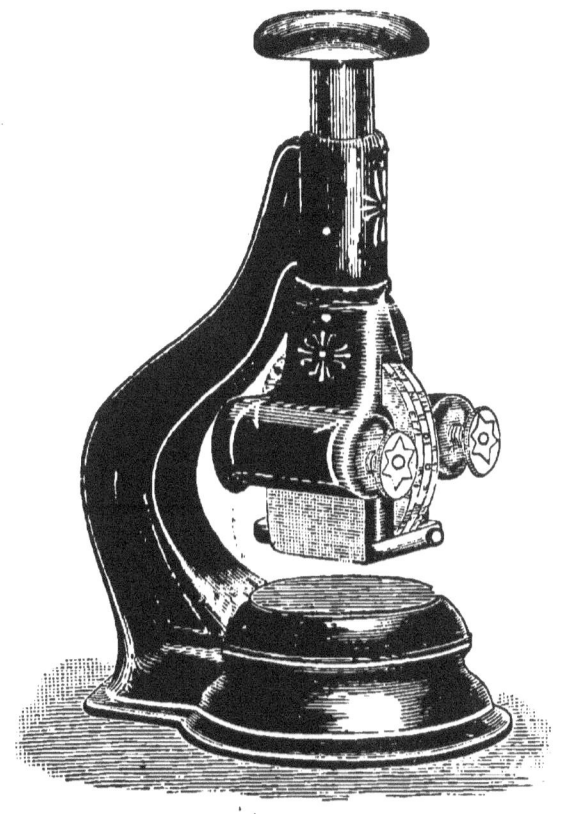

THIS DATING STAMP, WITH BRASS DIE ENGRAVED,
COMPLETE, $3.50.

◄NEW YORK STENCIL WORKS►
Stamp Manufacturers,
No. 100 NASSAU STREET, NEW YORK.

The Smith & Egge Mfg. Co.,
LAFAYETTE ST., cor. Allen, BRIDGEPORT, CONN.

Contractors with the U. S. Government for Mail Locks,

ALSO MANUFACTURERS OF

Sewing-Machine,
Piano and
Organ Locks,

U. S. Mail Locks,
Fine Brass Locks,

Sewing-Machine Locks,
Piano Locks,
Organ Locks,
Giant Padlocks.

SPECIAL LOCKS MADE TO ORDER FOR RAILROADS AND OTHERS.

Sewing - Machine Hardware,

Small Hardware.

Light • Metallic • Goods
MADE TO ORDER.

Basin & Bath Tub Chains,
Patented Inventions,
Tools, etc.

"Giant" Metal automatically made Sash Chain,
And the attachments required for hanging the Sash. Prices and Samples of Chain sent on application.

Adopted by the Commissioners for the new Capitol at Hartford, Ct., the new City Hall, Providence, R.I., and for new State, War and Navy Department Buildings at Washington, D.C., and other U.S. buildings.

The only suitable article to hang Plate Glass. Manufacturers of U. S. Mail Locks, Treasury Locks, "Giant," Seal and Register Padlocks; also "Giant" Drill Chucks—all Steel, strong, effective and simple in construction. "Jewett's" patented Double and Single acting Spring Butts, a new device and very strong at closing point

THE STAMFORD FOUNDRY CO.

STAMFORD, CT.

MANUFACTURERS OF

STOVES,

Cooking, Heating and Laundry Stoves, Parlor Stoves, Ship Stoves.

Gas Burner and Cylinder Castings.

RANGES,

Portable and Brick Set, for Families, Boarding Houses and Hotels.

WARM AIR FURNACES

SMALL AND LARGE.

A Great Variety of Patterns and Sizes.

SOLD BY DEALERS GENERALLY.

For the Finger Nails.   For the Feet.

CREAM VANOLA,   **OLIVINE,**
Pocket EMERY BOARD,   **PEDOLIN,**
ONGOLINE.   **DEODORIN.**

HANDSOME NAIL TOILET CASES, in fittings of Boxwood and Ivory, Hammered Silver or Copper, and Ivory.

Finger Nails Beautified in the most Artistic manner for $1.00, by four lady Manicures, under my instruction.

BITING, HANG AND BRITTLE NAILS CURED.

I give my personal attention to diseases of the Skin and Feet.

Dr. J. PARKER PRAY, Surgeon Chiropodist,
AND AMERICA'S FIRST MANICURE.

ONLY OFFICES:
NEW YORK: 38 West 23d Street, adjoining STERN BROS.
ALWAYS OPEN.   ESTABLISHED 1866.
SARATOGA: Arcade (Post Office Building) Rooms 10 and 12.
OPEN JULY 1st to SEPT. 1st.

Dr. J. PARKER PRAY'S
Perfection ✻ Manicure ✻ Goods.

THE OLDEST, MOST RELIABLE AND ONLY
PREPARATIONS HAVING A UNIVERSAL
SALE EVERYWHERE.

BEWARE OF INJURIOUS IMITATIONS.

◄ASK IN DRUG AND FANCY GOODS STORES FOR►

Dr. PRAY'S

PREPARATIONS—AND—ACCEPT NO OTHERS.

xxxvi   THOMPSON'S ADVERTISING DIRECTORY

The Judd Manufacturing Co.
101, 103 & 105 W. 36th St., N. Y.
WHOLESALE AND RETAIL DEALERS AND OUTFITTERS IN

Fine Athletic Goods

Lawn Tenis, Base Ball, Boxing Gloves, Foot Ball,

INDIAN CLUBS, DUMB BELLS,

☞Implements and Apparatus for all Field Sports, Gymnasium and House use. Exercising Apparatus of every description.

SPORTING CLOTHING A SPECIALTY.

AN ATHLETE'S ADVANTAGE — Get your goods at JUDD'S, who furnishes every item in the Profession. Thirty years' Professional experience. Full selections.

Automatic Bank Punch Co.
35 TEMPLE COURT, NEW YORK CITY.
Manufactory, York and Washington Streets, Brooklyn, N. Y.

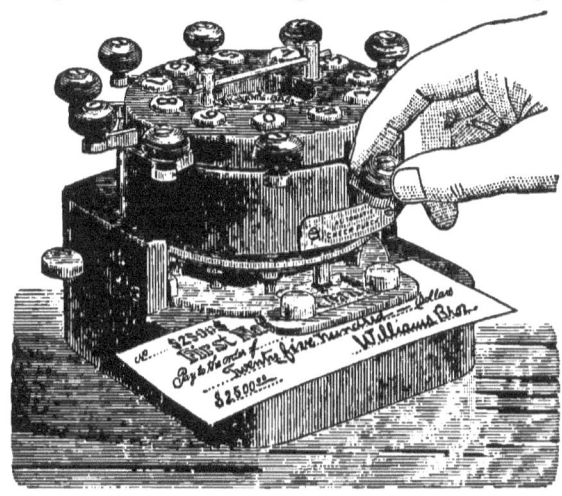

PRICE, - - $36.00

It is endorsed by the U. S. Treasury Department, New York Clearing House and Bank Experts as the safest means of preventing the amounts being changed. Anything short of Punching the figures out is a temptation and risk.

Now coming into universal use, and being adopted everywhere.

Automatic in operation, simple in construction, easy and rapid to operate; cannot be used·wrong; not liable to get out of order; fully guaranteed.

Machines may be ordered subject to examination, and returned if not satisfactory.

Send for Illustrated and Descriptive Circulars and Price-List.

THE AUTOMATIC BANK PUNCH; used and endorsed by such People as—

Wm. A. Camp, Manager N. Y. Clearing House; Morton, Bliss & Co., Bankers, New York; F. M Schaefer Brewing Co , New York; Winslow, Lanier & Co., New York; Knickerbocker Trust Co., New York; W. H. Schieffelin & Co., New York; First National Bank, Marshalltown, Ia.; Municipal Gas Light Co., New York; Equitable Insurance Co., New Eork; Equitable Gas Co., New York, and many others.

WATERMAN'S
"IDEAL" FOUNTAIN PEN

Asa L. Shipman's Sons, 10 Murray Street, N. Y.

Is four pieces of hard rubber : (1) the Cap which covers and protects the pen in the pocket; (2) the Handle, which holds the ink ; (3) the Point-section, which takes the pen ; and (4) the Feed-bar, which holds the pen in its place and carries the ink from the reservoir to the pen, using the same principle (capillary attraction), by a similar construction (a split of fissures), that the pen uses in conducting the ink to the paper, and is equally as certain.

The act of writing regulates the flow of ink, which is as free as from a dip pen, and more uniform.

It takes the ordinary gold or steel pens.

Your favorite pen can be used, and the character of your handwriting will be preserved.

It is the simplest, cleanest, readiest and most easily managed of all the fountain pens.

It has no machinery to be regulated.

When the cap is removed the pen is ready to write; when the writing is done the cap can be replaced and it is ready for the pocket.

It uses any ink, and holds enough to write continuously from 10 to 25 hours.

There are several sizes for the pocket and the desk.

PRICES:

For Holders, ... $2.25 to $4.50
Holders with Gold Pens. . 3.50 " 7.00

With each pen is given a certificate which warrants the holder for five years, and guarantees it to give satisfaction or the money will be refunded. It also contains a license under the patent which protects the user from all claims for infringements.

All people are cautioned against buying or using similar pens without getting therewith a license under the patent.

Patented Feb. 12 and Nov. 4, 1884.

ESTABLISHED 1856.   ONE PRICE ONLY.

J. LEACH,
Stationer, Printer
── AND ──
BLANK BOOK MANUFACTURER,

86 Nassau Street, New York.

Black, Blue, Carmine, Red, Copying & Violet Inks
Letter, Note, Foolscap, Bill and Legal Cap.

All SIZES of CASH BOXES. STANDARD, NATIONAL and SPRING-BACK DIARIES on Hand all the Year.

☞ All kinds of Esterbrook, Gillott's, Perry's, Spencerian, Egyptian and Washington Medallion Steel Pens. LEACH'S Falcon and Law Pens.

Fine Birthday Cards and Novelties.

HOTEL REGISTERS on hand and made to order. All kinds of Account Books made to order at the shortest notice.

SHRIVER'S
—NEW YORK—
COPYING PRESSES.

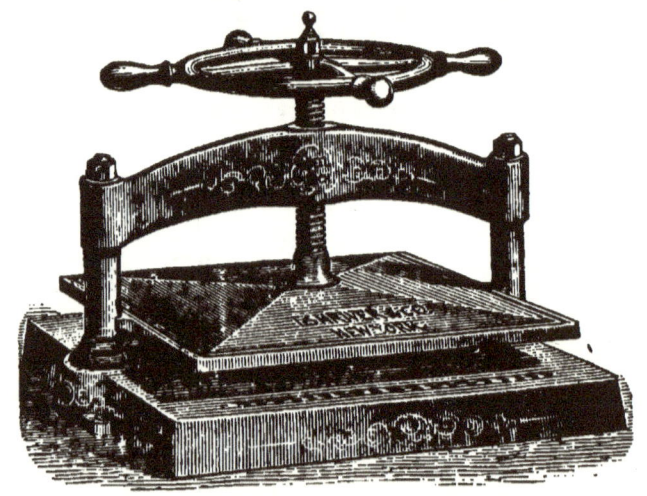

LARGE STEEL ARCH RAILROAD PRESS.
Platen, 22 x 24 inches.

T. SHRIVER & CO.
333 East 56th St., New York,

MANUFACTURERS OF

Copying Presses of all sizes for Railroad, Express and Transportation Companies, and for General Mercantile Use.

SEND FOR ILLUSTRATED PRICED CIRCULAR.

ESTABLISHED 1839.

THOMAS HOOPER,
⚜ PRACTICAL ⚜
PICTURE ∞ FRAMER,
DEALER IN

Mirrors, Gilt and Fancy Wood Mouldings, Oil Paintings, Engravings and Chromos,

WHOLESALE AND RETAIL.

OIL PAINTINGS AND ENGRAVINGS RESTORED.
OLD FRAMES RE-GILDED EQUAL TO NEW.

114 NASSAU STREET,
Bet. Ann and Beekman Sts.   NEW YORK.

C. HARTFIELD,
Successor to H. S. DANZIGER,
⟶PATENTEE AND MANUFACTURER OF⟵

MOTH'S ENEMY,
Indian Insect Powder,
— AND —
INVINCIBLE MAGNETIC PASTE,
WHOLESALE AND RETAIL,

No. 57 Bowery, New York.

☞ Orders taken for Clearing Houses and Ships of Bed Bugs, Water Bugs, Roaches, Moths, Fleas, &c.

BLUME & CO.

113 Water Street, New York,
SOLE IMPORTESS OF

Barry & Reynolds' London Prepared Cocoa,
English and Powdered Chicory,
B & C German Granulated Chicory,
Hauswaldt's, Seelig's & Franck's Paper Chicory.

ASK YOUR GROCER FOR

BEST FOR FAMILY USE.

NO HOUSEHOLD SHOULD BE WITHOUT IT.

Blume & Co. Sole Importers. N. Y.

PURE BLOOD!

The Greatest Blood Purifier *in the* World.

Dickinson's Alterative Remedies

They will cure Abscesses, Ulcers, Scrofula, Tumors, Erysipelas, Open Sores, Inflammation, Piles, Boils, Neuralgia, Dyspepsia, Sick Headache, Billiousness, Female Weakness, and all irregularities of the system and diseases of the blood.

These "Medicines," consisting of a BALSAM and OINTMENT, are perfectly safe, being purely vegetable, strengthen the system while they remove and cure disease. SEND FOR CIRCULAR.

GEO. K. DICKINSON, Sole Proprietor,

Office, 265 Main St., Room 4, HARTFORD, CONN.

STILES' GALVANIC OIL,
The Great Counter Irritant!
FOR SPRAINS, BURNS AND BRUISES.

"SURE CURE FOR RHEUMATISM."

For sale by Druggists everywhere. Price 25c., 50c. and $1.00 per Bottle.

Principal Office, 123 Leonard Street,

NEW YORK.

New York Conservatory of Music

LOCATED ONLY AT

No. 5 E. 14th St., 3d door east of 5th Ave.

Chartered in 1885. Empowered to award Diplomas and confer Degrees

BRANCHES TAUGHT.

Piano ✢ Singing ✢ Organ ✢ Harp ✢ Violin ✢ Violincello

ORCHESTRAL INSTRUMENTS.

Harmony, Composition, Counterpoint, Instrumentation

NORMAL CLASSES.

Operatic Classes, Chorus Classes, Church Choir and Concert Singing.

LANGUAGES.

French, German, Italian and Spanish,
Elocution, Oratory and Dramatic Art.
Drawing, Oil and Water Color Painting and Decoration.

A Special Training Course for Teachers.

TERMS:
- Classes of Three Pupils, $10 00 per Quarter.
- Classes of Two Pupils,   .   15 00 "   "
- Strictly Private Lessons, .   30 00 "   "

FREE ELEMENTARY CLASSES AND CLASS IN HARMONY, COMPOSITION AND SIGHT READING.

MONTHLY MUSICAL and ART RECEPTIONS.

Open Daily during the entire year. Quarters begin from date of Entrance.

AND BUYERS GUIDE. xlv

D. A. MAYER,
526 BROADWAY,

Importer of Hungarian Wines.

Tokay ✳ New York ✳ Budapest.

The only house in the United States where Hungarian Wines are sold which have been awarded *Medals* for *Purity and Superior Quality by the Centennial Commissioners*. **GENUINE TOKAY WINES A SPECIALTY.**—The medical fraternity of Europe recommend these Wines for their remedial properties, as also many eminent physicians of the City of New York and through- out the United States certify to their value as an ordinary tonic for strengthening the system of the convales- cent, and for their recuperative powers they are admitted to be a panacea for many of the "ills which flesh is heir to."

Prof. LIEBIG thus writes: "Wine—as a restorative, as a means of correction and compensation, where misproportion occurs in nutrition, and the organism is deranged in its operation, and as a means of protec- tion against transient organic disturbances—Wine is surpassed by no product of nature or art." And again he observes: "Wine is the universal medicine for the healthy as well as for the sick, for the infant or adult, and is as milk to the aged."

ATTENTION, HOTEL-KEEPERS!

Hines' Laundry Soap Powder

IS THE BEST AND CHEAPEST ARTICLE IN THE MARKET FOR ALL WASHING PURPOSES. ESPECIALLY ADAPTED FOR

LAUNDRY WORK • AND • SUMMER HOTELS.

Box of Fifty Pounds. $4.

MORISON & CO.

110 Water Street, - - Boston, Mass.

ELECTRIC LIGHTS

Small Lamps for Table and Office use that cost only one cent an hour to run, and will run ten hours.

CARRIAGE LAMPS, BICYCLE LAMPS, weighing only 13 oz.

LAMPS for TRAVELING on Country Roads; very powerful.

NIGHT LAMPS that can be called into action by simply pulling a string; no smell or danger.

ELECTRIC SCARF PINS.

FREDERICK LOWEY, - Manufacturer,

96 & 98 Fulton Street, New York.

Post Office Box 1322.

BOSTON ❧ BROWN ❧ BREAD.

ALL FIRST-CLASS HOTELS

———— SHOULD USE THE ————

Boston Brown Bread Mixture.

It contains the four properties of Four Royal Grains, and by the addition only of Milk or Water and a little Molasses, makes a delicious, spongy, brown loaf of genuine

Olden Time Boston Brown Bread.

Royal Breakfast Gems in fifteen minutes. Our Griddle Cakes are FIT FOR A KING.

Put up in 1, 2½ and 5 pound packages, and sold by all leading Grocers in the United States.

———— ●●●●●● ————

BOSTON CEREAL MF'G CO.,

Boston, Mass., U. S. A.

BASTINE'S
Flavoring Extracts

Are Strictly Pure and of the Finest Quality.

THEY ARE USED BY ALL THE BEST HOTELS AND FAMILIES THROUGHOUT THE COUNTRY.

MANUFACTURED BY

BASTINE & CO.

41 & 43 Warren Street, N. Y.

HOW TO BE BEAUTIFUL

The Secret has been Successfully Solved!

BY THE
Parfumerie,  Monte Christo.

TRADE MARK.
—— ESTABLISHED 1860. ——

Eugenie's Secret of Beauty!

It not only beautifies but purifies the complexion, also produces a brilliant transparency.
Satisfaction guaranteed or money refunded. Price, $1.50 per box.

Veloutine Face Powder.

Warranted the Best in the World, 50c. and $1 per box.

INDELIBLE LIQUID FACE ROUGE. Price $1.00 per bottle.
INDELIBLE LIQUID LIP ROUGE. Price $1 per bottle. Also our
BEAUTIFYING MASK, which is renowned throughout the world. Price (with accompanying preparations), $2, and an additional assortment of beautifying specialties.
MAMMARIAL BALM, for developing purposes. Price $1 per bot.
DEPILATORY POWDER, for removing superfluous Hair. Price $1.00 per bottle.
ADONINE, for dyeing instantaneously the Hair, Beard, Eyebrows and Eyelashes; light brown, brown, dark brown or black, without soiling the skin. Price, $1.50 per bottle. Also the
MAGIC HAIR TONIC. Price $1 per bottle.

Hair Cutting and Curling on premises by the best French Artistes. Front pieces dressed while you wait, 25c. each.

Goods sent C. O. D., with the privilege of returning, at my expense, till satisfied.

L. SHAW,
54 W. 14th Street, near 6th Avenue, New York.

ESTABLISHED 1830.

JAMES Y. WATKINS & SON,

MANUFACTURERS OF

Hotel & Restaurant

KITCHEN WARE,

Ice Cream Freezers, Moulds,

BAKERS AND CONFECTIONERS' UTENSILS.

We make a Specialty of furnishing the Pastry and Baking Departments of Hotels and Steamers.

No. 16 Catharine St.,
NEW YORK.

NEW IMPROVED HIGH ARM
AVERY SEWING MACHINE.

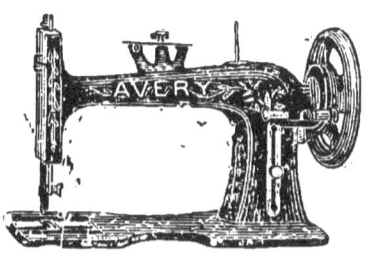

Self-Threading Machine, Self-Threading Cylinder Shuttle, Loose Pulley for Winding Bobbin. Non-Fatiguing, Light Running, Noiseless, Rapid !!

" NEW AUTOMATIC TENSION."

Patent adjustable Band Wheel and Treadle, with Steel Centres.

No Friction! No Noise! No Wear! No "Tantrums" nor getting out of order. Always ready to sew the finest or heaviest goods, giving entire satisfaction.

Avoiding Gears, Cogs, Cams and Levers, and substituting therefor an entirely New Mechanical Principle and Movement. A radical improvement seen at a glance, and greatly desired by all. Automatic, Direct and Perfect Action in every part. No Transferred Motion.

———*ADDRESS*———

Avery Machine Co.,
812 BROADWAY, NEW YORK.

PIANO AND ORGAN STOOLS,

MERIDEN, CONN

JOHN C. HAM
MANUFACTURER OF
Fine Carriages, Jerome & Village Carts,

Most reliable House to purchase of. ★ Established Forty-eight Years.
VICTORIAS, "T" CARTS, BROUGHAMS, COUPES, SURRYS,
FINE BUGGIES. COUPE ROCKAWAYS. LANDAUS,
LANDAULETTES, DOCTOR WAGONS A SPECIALTY.

Samples of every style of Carriage and Cart at our Warerooms. Satisfactory Prices. We only make warranted work.

No. 27 WOOSTER STREET, NEW YORK CITY, N. Y.

FREDERICK D. FUCHS,
Commission ◦ Merchant.
SOLE AGENT IN THE UNITED STATES FOR

Furlaud Freres & Co's Chateauneuf Pres Cognac,

No. 5 BROAD STREET,
BOSTON

GEO. W. JOPSON,

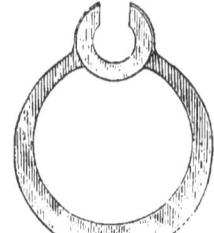

MANUFACTURER OF

PATENT
KEY RINGS

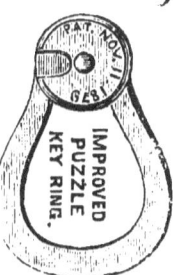

No. 153 State Street, Meriden, Conn.

MME. B. ZITTEL'S
MANICURE PARLOR.
12 EAST 14th STREET.

MANNSINA, the Instantaneous Polish for the Finger Nails, applied free of charge.
　MANNSINA CREAM, the most delicate Preparation for the Skin.
　MANNSINA JELLY and **MANNSINA POWDER** for Sale.

MME. ZITTEL'S PERFUMED POCKETS.

ECLIPSE CHAMPAGNES,
DRY AND EXTRA DRY.
Arpad Haraszthy & Co.

These Champagnes are the result of Twenty Years of preparation, and the only Champagnes produced on the Pacific Coast, and EQUAL in EVERY RESPECT to the FOREIGN.

Quarts, $14.85 ; Pints, $16.65.

A DISCOUNT ALLOWED TO HOTELS.

◄ CLARETS ►
Superior Clarets, - at - $45, $50, $55 and $65.
For Casks of 60 galls.

◄ SHERRIES ►
Fine COOKING and TABLE Sherries for Hotels.

FRED'K WM. LUTTGEN,
SOLE AGENT,
51 Warren Street, - - NEW YORK.

Brandy and Port in Cases for Medicinal Use.

WATCHMAN'S
New Improved Time Detector,
WITH SAFETY LOCK ATTACHMENT.

The Safety Lock Attachment is a true guard on the Watch, preventing the Watchman from tampering with it successfully.

IMPORTANT AND INVALUABLE FOR ALL CONCERNS EMPLOYING WATCHMEN.

Send ✧ for ✧ Circular.

Patented 1875, 1876, 1877, 1880, 1881 and 1882. Beware of Infringements.

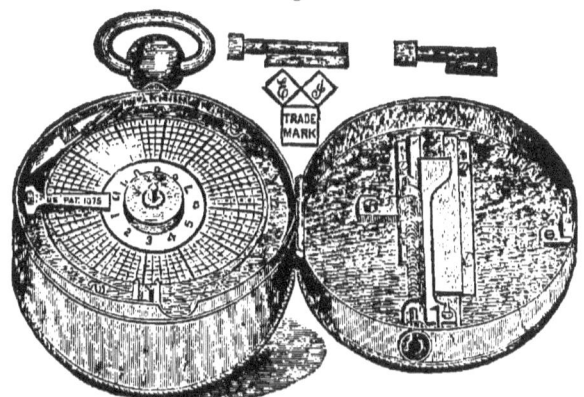

This instrument is supplied with 12 different keys for 12 different stations. It contains all modern improvements against the old style, and this is the only complete instrument.

1876—Highest Award and Medal of Honor at the Centennial Exhibition, for Portability, Security and general adaptation to the purposes intended.——1877, '78, '79—Medals for Excellence and Superiority, at the American Institute.——1881—Award at the International Cotton Exposition in Atlanta.——1883—At the National Exposition for Railway Appliances at Chicago, the ONLY Medal for the most Complete and Perfect Instrument.

E. IMHAUSER,
P. O. Box 2875.   212 Broadway, N. Y.

Guaranteed not to have, nor never to have had, any connection ——— with other Patentees. ———

MURTAUGH'S
Genuine Dumb Waiters and General Hand Hoisting Establishment,
145 & 147 EAST 42d STREET, NEW YORK.

Carriage and Safety Invalid Elevators a Specialty. Repairing and Altering at the Shortest Notice. Established 1855.

James Murtaugh & Co.

HORTON'S
ICE CREAM
MADE FROM PURE CREAM.
THE BEST AND MOST POPULAR ICE CREAM IN THE WORLD.

Horton's Patent Super-frozen Bricks of Ice Cream a specialty. Will keep hard one hour.

DEPOTS
305 Fourth Avenue,   75 Chatham Street,
    1288 Broadway,   110 E. 125th St., N. Y.
And 453 Fulton Street, Brooklyn.

W. J. RIGNEY.   JUSTUS WOLFF

RIGNEY & WOLFF,
Analytical and Technical Chemists,
Office and Laboratory, 109 Wall St., N. Y.

We respectfully invite consultation on questions of Chemical or Technical Nature, relating to the Manufactures, Arts and Sciences; also Chemico-Legal Questions. Analysis made of all kinds of Commercial and Agricultural Products. Examinations of Food Products and Beverages.

THE AMERICAN

Encaustic Tiling Co.

---LIMITED.---

PATENTEES AND MANUFACTURERS OF ALL KINDS
OF PLAIN AND FIGURED

TILES

*For the Floor and External Decoration
of Churches, Halls, Public
Buildings, Etc.*

116 West Twenty-third Street,

NEW YORK.

B. FISCHER, President.
GEO. R. LANSING, Treas.
WM. G. FLAMMER, Secy.

TELEPHONE CALL,
415 21st Street.